"Sue's story is truly inspirational!"

Layne Beachley – Seven-time world champion surfer

"Such a wonderful blend of strategy and storytelling. Don't let another day go by without discovering and uncovering the person you are destined to be so you may feel fulfilled and leave a lasting impression on those around you."

Julie Cross – Motivational speaker

"Sue's uplifting personal story and practical advice will inspire you on your entrepreneurial journey. She has learnt how to overcome and succeed."

Lisa McInnes-Smith – Global keynote speaker

IMPRESS *ario*

Present and Promote the Star Within You

SUE CURRIE

Published in Australia in 2017 by Sue Currie

Web: www.suecurrie.com.au

www.impressario.com.au

© Sue Currie 2017

The moral right of the author has been asserted.

ISBN 9780646934235 (paperback)

NATIONAL LIBRARY OF AUSTRALIA

A catalogue record for this book is available from the National Library of Australia

Disclaimer

Contents

Dedication   vii

Acknowledgements   ix

Introduction   1

PART ONE – Behind the Scenes

1   A Star is Born   7

2   The Script   29

3   Star Quality   41

PART TWO – Prepare for the Role

4   The Rehearsal   55

5   The Costumes   71

6   The Production   93

PART THREE – Showtime

7   Marketing You   105

8   Publicist to the Star   121

9   The Show Must Go On   143

Conclusion   155

Bibliography   159

About the Author   163

To Danièle and Sandra: the "Mums".

Steve, a loving father.

Naomi, our daughter and Connor, our grandson.

And to the other main man in my life: Peter, thank you.

Acknowledgements

This book didn't just happen overnight. For me, it has been a start–stop process and took much longer than originally planned. I could not have written it without the loving support and encouragement of my friends and family. Most importantly, Naomi Miller, who I am proud to say is my daughter, was very instrumental in helping me bring this project to fruition. We have now been best of friends for over twenty-five years and I am so fortunate to have her in my life.

Introduction

IMPRESS*ario* – Present and Promote the Star Within You

IMPRESS*ario* is the title of my book which involves a play on the word "impresario": the producer or director of a theatrical production and the word "impress". In this book, I focus on how to make an impression, make your mark, and be the person you are destined to be. Through reading IMPRESS*ario*, you will understand how combining these two elements will produce a personal brand and a business that will be successful for you and will fulfil your ambitions.

^**Impress** – affect, influence, characteristic, mark, imprint, stamp, impression, effect produced on feeling, impress idea on person or the mind.

^**Impresario** – organiser of public entertainment especially opera or concert, theatrical entrepreneur, producer, press agent and business manager.

In IMPRESS*ario* I also share my own personal journey. Any theatrical production has its share of dramas and IMPRESS*ario* does too as I share my background story. This is the first time I've told my story of overcoming the heartache of an early teenage pregnancy to eventually reaching the point of achieving a successful career. It is also an account of what I've experienced and observed from others, and about what it takes to succeed on your entrepreneurial journey.

The book is not just about my story. It is also designed to be a practical and useful guide for you. I provide you with tools, tips and plans to implement so you can grow a memorable brand and successful business. My book progresses through three areas: like an opera impresario or theatre director, your path will go from: (1) Behind the Scenes to (2) Preparing for the Role and then on to (3) Showtime.

PART ONE – We take a look BEHIND THE SCENES to understanding your personal brand. Who you are, how to get to know yourself a little bit better and understand how you portray your brand image and come across to others. Through practical examples and exercises, you will learn about impression management, including how to understand the perceptions that other people have about you. You will also learn how to explore your personality, characteristics and strengths, as well as how to bring out your star quality.

Most of us face struggles in our daily life that may hinder our progress and prevent us from achieving our goals. In this book, I share my story of sorrow and loss and the realisation that, although your background story contributes to it, it doesn't have to shape your future direction. We've all had stuff happen to us – that's just life.

I also hope to inspire you to have a go, no matter what. You have the opportunity to achieve the business, work or career that you want to create. You can be the IMPRESS*ario* of your own life and business.

PART TWO – We PREPARE FOR THE ROLE and review the practical steps you need to take to plan and prepare before you get to realise your production. Rarely does instant success happen. Through many auditions, try outs, being persistent and well prepared you may, after a number of years, become an "overnight success".

This section also looks at the significant part "costume" plays in presenting and enhancing you as the main character in your production. This is an area I am passionate about and part of my background experience that I want you to appreciate. I discuss the important role visual image plays and how your personal brand is expressed through your own unique style and what you wear.

PART THREE – It's now SHOWTIME! What does it take to get the show on the road? On the entrepreneurial journey, we're all in the business of marketing, whether it is ourselves or our business. Very rarely does a major production get noticed unless a marketing and public relations campaign takes place. Knowing how to manage and implement a personal marketing strategy will ensure you gain attention. This section includes a personal brand communication plan to help you stand out from the crowd. With my many years of experience in promoting stars, businesses and personalities, I know what it takes to become known, be seen and be heard.

Having been on an entrepreneurial journey for most of my working life, I wanted to write this book to inspire you to keep going and strive to do what you love doing every day. Most of us change direction many times throughout our working life; sometimes intentionally but often unintentionally. There are peaks and troughs; that's just life in our working world. Today, many people are forgoing the traditional route of working for one or more employers to tread the unknown path of self-employment. Our working life is a lot longer these days and it's fun. So keep going and make your working life an exciting part of what you do.

In my personal experience working with brands and celebrities in a career spanning over thirty years, I have seen many successes and failures. One attribute that has stood out for me is belief. Believing you can do it, you will do it, and that is why you should do it: to be the star you're destined to be will underpin your success. I believe we can all be intentional in our pursuit of a successful business or career.

It is not about ego or being the most impressive person out there. It is about taking a step-by-step approach to creating your own future. Yes, you will make an impact; yes, you will impress; yes, you will create a production which is your personal brand and business if you follow the steps I suggest.

I hope you enjoy reading IMPRESS*ario* and I wish you the best in your entrepreneurial journey. Begin now and step into your personal brand of success.

^ **Sources of definitions:**

The Australian Pocket Oxford Dictionary © Oxford University Press, 1976.

Roget's Thesaurus © Crown Publishers, Inc. 1979

PART ONE

Behind the Scenes

One

A Star is Born

"If you are looking for something, don't go sit on the sea-shore and expect it to come and find you; you must search, search, search with all the stubbornness in you!"

– Constantin Stanislavski

The year was 1984 and I was about to graduate from the Ensemble Studios acting school after three long years. My fellow thespians and I were gathered in one of the classrooms of the old Independent Theatre in Sydney, where the studio acting classes were being held. There were about twenty of us sitting around in a circle. We'd been together as students for three years, and although we knew each other well, there was a certain amount of trepidation in the room because we were about to be exposed. Not in the literal sense, but our secret, inner self was about to be revealed.

That moment was when I first came across the concept of personal branding, although at the time I had no idea what that meant. My acting course had been a three-year part-time undertaking and was a truly remarkable experience.

Yes, at the time my goal was to be an actor and I did follow that path for a few years. But everything I learned in that course has since stood me in good stead in my work, career and life today.

An actor's job is to take on a character and portray them as truthfully as possible and, in doing so, make that person believable to the audience.

We studied the Stanislavski Method school of acting and often did exercises where we had to recreate past experiences or use other sensory methods to help us really get into the personality or place of the character we were portraying.

Many actors play character roles and are fabulous at playing parts from a diva to a downtrodden divorcee – just look at Meryl Streep. However, often actors are cast very close to "type".

In my final year, we undertook this exercise with our classmates to discover more about how we came across to others. The idea was to develop a better understanding of our "type" – what characteristics and traits came through from our own innate personality and what style of role we would be best suited to. This experience occurred more than thirty years ago but it was so powerful that it has remained with me ever since. I still share with clients and in workshop exercises what I discovered during that time.

I clearly remember being in the classroom when our teacher asked us to choose words to describe ourselves; adjectives and phrases that we thought best summed up ourselves and how we came across to others. We were given a few examples of famous actors and we chose words to describe them, such as charismatic and confident. Once we had done that, we made a list of twenty or so of our words. One by one, we were asked to leave the room. It was my turn and I was quite excited to think about all the fabulous things my friends would say about me. But I was in for a big surprise. Although my very obvious public traits clearly connected with what I had written, there were also words and perceptions from others that were completely new to me. I was quite astonished and a bit upset by some of the perceptions that others had of me.

What I didn't realise at the time was that we had performed a simple psychology test using the Johari window. This process was devised by two psychologists Harry Ingham and Joseph Luft (Joe and Harry – Johari) in the 1950s and it forms the basis for many well-known psychometric personality tests and personal branding exercises that are used today.

As an actor, it is important to understand your true personality and to be able to bring out hidden aspects of who you are in order to authentically play a role and portray a character. In life, it is also a valuable tool to understand how we come across to others and what positive aspects of our personality shine through. By being clear about the various aspects of our personality and behaviour, as well as the personal image and reputation that others may have of us, we can start to realise some of our untapped potential.

While I'm not a psychologist, I am very interested in human behaviour and how we manage the impressions we (often unknowingly) share with the world. Therefore, I think the Johari window model is a good tool for making the process of understanding ourselves a little clearer.

Who are you?

The Johari Window

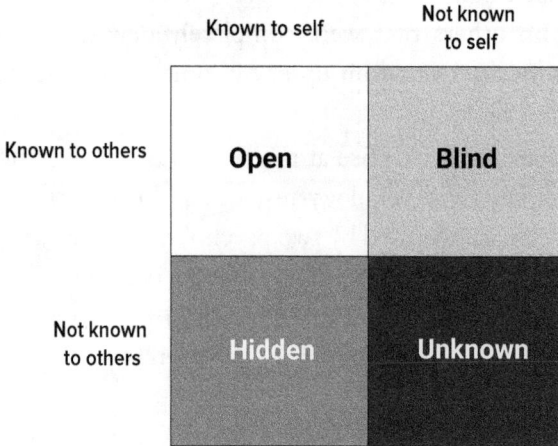

	Known to self	Not known to self
Known to others	**Open**	**Blind**
Not known to others	Hidden	Unknown

The Johari window model demonstrates four elements of your personality and inner being. The first part is the **Open Self** – the part of you that everyone sees. This is the side of yourself that you show openly to the outside world. This area includes your appearance, hairstyle and grooming: the obvious physical aspects of how you appear. It also includes your visual image: how you style yourself, including which photos of yourself you choose to share. It is the first impression you make and is how others sum you up instantly. It also represents your people skills – how you interact with people, conversational ability, social graces, and your customer and client service. It encapsulates what sort of instant impact you have on others and how people surmise who you are.

The second element of the square is the opposite to your public self. It is the **Hidden Self** – the hidden image. It is the part only you know about and incorporates how you feel about many things and different aspects of your life. Areas to look at here are your attitudes, self confidence level, your past private experiences that you may not want to share, and your anxieties and fears. These are usually the areas you don't want others to know about you. Examining your private inner self also reveals your goals, dreams, hopes and ambitions. Perhaps you haven't realised a secret ambition because your past experiences have led to uncertainty and fear. Taking stock of what your private self is indicating will help to reveal your way forward to becoming the star of your own destiny.

The **Blind Self** – we all have our blind spots, and these fill another quarter of the Johari window model. These are parts of our personality that others see yet we cannot see ourselves. It includes your reputation and what other people think and say about you that you're unaware of. It might be that people perceive you to be a kind and very helpful person but you're not really aware of it because it is your innate nature to help people. This is one lovely characteristic that my husband has. He is always very hospitable and helpful to people but brushes this off by saying, "It's not hard". It isn't to him because that is very much a part of his personality; however, other people struggle to even say something nice.

What do people say about you? In my case, when I was being analysed by my acting school friends, I thought they'd say I was open and friendly. I had written that down on my sheet of paper; however, my acting colleagues had described me as being a bit aloof and mysterious. I didn't realise that "stand offish" was how I came across to others. Maybe you see yourself as shy and a bit quiet, but others see you as lacking in confidence. This window is exciting because it always explores aspects of your personality that you don't already know about yourself.

I was discussing personal reputation at a briefing with a client and he gave an example of someone in his office who was smart and very good at his job. However, nobody wanted to deal with this person because he was a "misery guts". Let's hope that people don't say that about you! You want people to be talking about you, but not for all the wrong reasons.

The fourth quadrant of the Johari window is the really exciting part: the **Unknown Self**, which is the untapped potential that is hidden from you and others. This includes all of the things we aren't aware about ourselves and that we haven't tapped into.

These parts of yourself may be called into action in a crisis, or they may be brought to life through further self-reflection on your hopes and dreams.

By looking at these four areas, we can start to uncover our true personality and our uniqueness. What is it that makes us special and how can we realise this potential? The ultimate aim of being an IMPRESS*ario* is you want to make a name for yourself in whatever domain you choose.

In order to determine who we are and what we want to achieve, the first step is to understand ourselves better. By working with the four areas of our Johari window we can find out what kind of personality and ambitions we have, the impression others have of us, and how we can reach our full potential.

Let me give you an example of why it's a good idea to better understand your blind and unknown selves. One time I was in a coaching session with a client – a senior female executive – who was brilliant at her job and a dedicated worker but, much to her dismay and bewilderment, after ten years of loyal service at the one company she had been let go. She didn't understand why, as not only had she performed her tasks well, she also led a large team that had delivered on-target every month. However, it turned out that there were two reasons why she had been made redundant. Firstly, every time she was asked to present to a group of people or put forward an important proposal to the leadership team she almost had a panic attack, so more senior staff felt that she didn't demonstrate the necessary leadership qualities required in her role. Secondly, she liked to "party hard" at work functions, to the annoyance and sometimes embarrassment of her boss. Had she been clear about how the senior executives saw her, she would no doubt have taken the necessary steps to overcome these behaviours.

The untapped potential in her unknown self might have included learning presentation skills and being able to fully assume a leadership role by overcoming her lack of confidence and fear about public speaking. As I previously mentioned, I'm not a psychologist, but perhaps her lack of confidence was also why she liked to have too many drinks at social events. With greater knowledge of her "blind self" and her reputation, she may have been able to remedy these two issues and avert her subsequent redundancy.

What do you want to be known for?

My acting studies stood me in good stead when I later decided to pursue a career in television. I had gained confidence through performing live on stage in plays, learned how to use my voice through speech coaching and had an understanding of how to work in front of the camera. This experience also built on the period I had previously spent modelling. To a certain extent, I was familiar with being onstage: strutting catwalks and modelling clothes, posing in front of the camera at fashion shoots and appearing in television commercials. In the early years of my career, I'd also had a brief stint on television as a weather girl. However, by this point, I had reached the end of my modelling career – possibly having a mid-life crisis in my late 20s! That is what prompted me to study acting and to ultimately pursue a career in television.

I applied to a number of television stations, auditioning for weather presenting roles, news reading and hosting positions. Eventually, I did land a role as the newsreader for RVN2 in Wagga Wagga, a regional area of New South Wales in Australia. It was a great start to what would end up being a ten-year career in television broadcasting.

Working in regional media was a wonderful learning experience and one I would recommend to anyone pursuing that career path. Not only was I presenting the nightly news live at 6.00 pm, during the day I was working in the newsroom helping out with a few news stories, watching how they were reported, filmed and edited. Even though I was not a trained journalist, it was an invaluable lesson in understanding what made news and how it all worked. I also hosted and produced a Morning Show.

It sounds very glamorous and "big time" but, in reality, I was "it" – the person who was responsible for finding people to interview for stories on air, deciding on some sort of schedule or theme for the episodes, and hosting the program (which we recorded three days a week). However, it was lots of fun and I learned as I went along through trial and error. I met some wonderful local people from all walks of life, as well as touring actors and authors.

One of the things I observed while working with the journalists was their use of words and phrasing when writing a story, particularly when they described a well-known personality, business person or sportsperson. When writing about someone, journalists and writers are able to paint a picture in our mind about that person through the use of descriptive words, adjectives and phrases. When you read a magazine or watch a TV report, consider what words are used to describe someone and how you form an instant opinion about that person based on this description.

Exercise: Identify your brand personality words

As an IMPRESS*ario* you are the personality. What adjectives would you use if you were a journalist and writing a story about you? How would you describe that person?

As an exercise, open up a magazine or newspaper and select a few famous personalities who are featured. What words come to mind instantly about those people? What is your observation or perception of a sports star or businessperson? We form an impression of other people relatively quickly and believe we have an understanding of their character, generally because of the way in which they are portrayed in the media. So who are you and how would you describe yourself?

Write down a list of words you think describe you well. All the wonderful, positive qualities you know you have! You may also identify words and adjectives that describe your hidden self that are not necessarily those you want to broadcast to everyone. Included in this chapter is a list of some words that may also describe you. Make your list of all the "you" personality words.

What about your passions?

Another clue to discovering your personal brand is to really think about the activities that inspire you; the things that you like to do and why. When you consider some of the things you really love doing, what is the feeling you get from that?

Let's set aside time for a moment to consider your skills and talents; not just those you bring to your role but what inspires you to jump out of bed every day with enthusiasm. Hopefully you already do that and your work does inspire you. However, if that's not the case, then by developing your understanding of your passions and the pastimes you enjoy, you will be able to incorporate some of these attributes into what you do. What is it that you truly love doing and why?

As an example, I love the beach – feeling the warmth of the sunlight on my skin (without sun baking) then diving through the waves into the ocean. Feeling the cool water is refreshing and energising for me. Long walks along the beach, seeing the sun come up or at sunset watching the sun go down, observing the changing colours of the sky, the smell of the ocean, the space and the freedom. All those elements of the beach I love and it makes me feel invigorated. I need to have that energetic, invigorating feeling and express that in my work to be happy. As a result of those feelings, "bright energy" is a term I would list as one of my personal brand characteristics.

Other activities I love are singing and dancing. Okay, I am not very good at either of these activities, even though I did jazz ballet and singing lessons as part of my acting course. However, if given the chance I'll do both with gay abandon. *Glee* was a favourite TV show of mine. I love any kind of performance: theatre musicals, great concerts, good TV drama, fabulous films, comedy and talk shows. You name it, performance inspires me. If I'm having an "off" day I can just take myself to the movies and emerge at the end feeling inspired. So clearly, throughout my career there has been an aspect of performance involved, whether it has been me actually on stage or helping others through roles such as television entertainment publicist or assisting CEOs to make a great Town Hall speech. Perhaps this personal attribute stemmed from a very young age when I was about six. One of my early memories is being on stage at Myer Melbourne in a line-up of equally young girls, wearing a pretty dress my mother had sewn for me. She had entered into a dressmaking competition and I was modelling her creation. Mind you she did tell me that I spent most of my time up on stage talking (let's just say communicating!). Communication and performance have always been part of my personal brand.

Are you beginning to see a theme here? Invigoration, bright energy, communication, performance, are words I'd record in my "you" passion words list. They are a result of understanding my passions and the feeling I have when I'm engaged in these pastimes.

Exercise: Identify your passion words

What topics excite you so much that you could talk about them endlessly or would make you tune into a TV program focused on these topics? What pastimes, activities and hobbies are you engaged in?

I want you to take a few moments now to think about the activities you love that inspire you and motivate you. And, most importantly, why do you like them? Is there a particular feeling or essence that emanates from you when you are enraptured? Identify and write down those words that describe the emotion you experience when you are engaged in your passions.

How do others see you?

Referring to my earlier examples of receiving feedback from my acting colleagues and the executive whose reputation resulted in redundancy, are you aware of the perception others may have of you and the reputation you currently have? To delve further into understanding perceptions, your reputation and what others think of you, it is a good idea to ask for feedback from your family, work colleagues and friends. I know this can be a bit daunting; however, it will give you valuable insight into the "blind self" area of your Johari window.

By getting an overview from a cross-section of people, you will observe common descriptors emerging that define your personality. Now don't worry – this won't be all bad. I know you're likely to be thinking, "I don't want to find out what people think of me!" However, by asking trusted confidantes to give you their honest appraisal, you will gain true insight about yourself.

Exercise: Determine the perceptions others have of your personal brand

Here's how to do it. List down six people's names: a mix of work colleagues, family and friends. You could also add employers; clients or customers you may have. Send them an email explaining that you are on a quest to improve your work and/or business position by understanding your current situation. Tell them you are contacting them to seek comments in order to understand your reputation and how you come across to others. Ask if it would be okay to call them and have a ten to fifteen-minute chat about their feedback so that you can develop and progress your personal brand. Suggest they let you know the best time and number to contact them on. Thank them in advance for their assistance.

When you do make contact, here are some questions you could ask:

- Please choose several words and adjectives to describe how you perceive my personal brand – both positive and negative.
- What would you say are my greatest strengths?
- What do you believe are my weaknesses?
- What do you believe I do well in my work and also not so well?

Thank you for your input so far. I'm really seeking candid feedback so is there anything else you would like to add?

You will get enough information from these few questions to take note of any recurring words or themes that keep coming up. In addition, look for words that may elicit an emotional connection. Are they "delighted" by you or "inspired"?

Once you have this information, check any performance reviews you may have had at work and if there are any common threads. Through this research, you should get more clarity on your clients' or employers' requirements from you and how people perceive you.

Now if you are really too uncomfortable to seek comment from others, you could send an email to your contacts and tell them the name of a trusted advisor or friend who will be in touch on your behalf. (Ask your trusted friend to do this for you, first of course!) – and again thank them for their assistance.

The following list of words may be used as a guideline to complete the Johari window. Select the words you would use and, if need be, ask your peers to select from this list also.

LIST OF PERSONALITY WORDS
Able, Accepting, Adaptable
Bold, Brave
Calm, Caring, Cheerful, Clever, Complex, Confident
Dependable, Dignified
Extroverted, Energetic
Friendly
Giving
Happy, Helpful
Idealistic, Independent, Ingenious, Intelligent, Introverted
Kind, Knowledgeable
Logical, Loving
Mature, Modest
Nervous
Observant, Organised
Patient, Powerful, Proud
Quiet
Reflective, Relaxed, Religious, Responsive
Searching, Self-assertive, Self-conscious, Sensible, Silly, Shy, Sentimental, Smart, Spontaneous, Sympathetic
Tense, Trustworthy
Wise, Witty, Warm

Exercise: Complete your Johari window

By now you will have compiled a list of words describing the perceptions others have of you. Now check this list of words against your own list of adjectives and words about yourself and your personality, and also the words about your passions to see what common themes, phrases or words emerge. Cross reference to find out which words from other people match up with your list and then circle those. You're starting to get more insight now into your true personality and how others see you. You can now start to fill in your own Johari window.

- Adjectives and words that have been selected by both you and the people you receive feedback from are placed into the Open Self quadrant.
- Adjectives selected only by you, but not by any of your peers, are placed into the Hidden Self quadrant. This is where you also place words about your dreams, desires and fears.
- Adjectives that have not been selected by you but are selected by your peers are placed into Blind Self.
- In the Unknown Self quadrant, you will make note of the gaps between Open, Hidden and Blind Self and what areas you need to focus on to realise your untapped potential.

Perhaps some negative attitudes or behaviour traits are now becoming apparent. Take note of some of these areas that you may need to modify. It can be hard to self-reflect and also to absorb this feedback, but it is invaluable to really understand yourself better. Ask yourself and others all the questions you need to complete the four squares of your Johari window. Do this audit to uncover your characteristics, beliefs, goals and passions.

The idea is that you work on your Hidden Self by looking at some of those hidden and private areas you need to improve. What do you want to achieve and what do you want to project to others by building on your strong innate characteristics?

Next look at your Open Self – how others see you – and then uncover some of the Blind Self. This is also where you will start to see the well-regarded aspects of yourself that shine through.

You need to tap into some of these areas; once you're satisfied that the personal brand image you're projecting is working well for you, then you can start to uncover your Unknown Self and unlock some of your unrealised potential.

What we've looked at during this exercise is a snapshot of where you are now. Who you think you are and what others believe about you up to this point. The untapped potential is what we want to delve into in order to bring out your true gifts.

What sets you apart?

It's now time to determine what you are good at or what you do differently: how to understand your unique set of skills and talents. You want to be able to stand out as a "brand" and be known for that one thing that will set you apart. Well-known examples of product brands include Volvo which is known for safety, Mercedes Benz for luxury, Woolworths are "the fresh food people". People brands include Stefan, the millionaire hairdresser; Jamie Oliver: chef, TV personality and author; or Michelle Bridges who is one of Australia's leading fitness gurus.

Of course, there are many examples of safe cars, fresh food outlets, chefs, hairdressers and fitness trainers. So why do these particular brands stand out? What's the answer and the formula for these success stories? Perhaps it is simply recognising and being very good at what you do and pursuing your passion?

In the case of Michelle Bridges – when she started out she was simply a fitness trainer but she worked hard to learn her trade. She started in the industry at an early age, running exercise classes during her school years at weekends and during holidays at a local squash centre. Michelle then went on to undertake a degree as a fitness instructor and trainer, became a Les Mills Pump class master instructor and was named Australian Fitness Leader of the Year in 2004. She was good at what she did, as well as having the credentials and lots of experience. At the time, these criteria were simply her point of difference.

For supermodel Elle Macpherson, it was her amazing figure that launched her career. She became known as "The Body" and graced many magazine covers wearing nothing more than a skimpy bikini. Elle also designed an underwear range and has maintained her body image and brand throughout her long career. Kylie Minogue – arguably Australia's leading pop princess – had singing talent. Greg ("The Great White Shark") Norman was a talented golfer. All of these individuals had raw talent; however, as their careers progressed, they developed other skills which enabled them to grow as business people and brands, and to really move on with their career goals.

Perhaps your true talent or gift is not evident to you right now. Nevertheless, write down a few sentences about the traits you think you currently offer and why these may be important or beneficial for others. For instance, a fitness trainer contributes to people becoming healthy and fitter. A hairdresser helps people to be well groomed and feel attractive. A sportsman inspires and motivates junior sports people to do their best.

Try to delve into your talents a bit further. Is there anything unique, a particular concept or idea that can set you apart from others? Are you tapping into a new idea or a major trend in your field and moving to the forefront of it? What is the creative element that might be coming through? Certainly, personal branding is not a new concept. Tom Peters – a well-known USA management and leadership consultant and author – is credited with starting the personal branding movement, when he first wrote about it in a *Fast Company* magazine article in 1997. Other people then followed his lead with their own individual approach to personal branding which, in turn, pushed this concept into the limelight. Is there a way of re-branding or re-framing what you do to make it sound new or more interesting? For example, many image consultants now call themselves stylists as it is a term that sounds more modern and mainstream.

You might have a special talent, skill or attribute that sets you apart. However, simply being really good at what you do may be your shining trait.

Yes, we all have a gift, a purpose, a reason for being. Maybe you just don't know what your gift or purpose is yet. We'll get to that later on. For now, just consider what excites you and what you're drawn to.

Once I was watching a TV talk show during which the famous comedian Billy Connelly was being interviewed. He was asked by the host what advice he would give his children about their future careers. Billy Connelly said, "See what you're drawn to. What shop windows do you look at? What magazines or books or activities appeal to you? What fascinates you? They are the things you should be doing".

Your personal brand statement

By now you should have a deeper understanding of your personality, as well as others' perceptions of you. Next, you can combine this awareness with your passions, skills and talents, and work towards writing a personal brand statement. Your personal brand statement should be as clear as possible; it's anchored in your passion and what attributes you bring to the world. It is an internal process. Later, you may turn it into a business brand tag line if that is relevant. However, for now, this is an internal communication. After all, business is personal and that's part of the reason for doing this exercise: we bring our personal nature into everything we do ... our work and our play. It's so much a part of us. So how do you write your personal brand statement?

Exercise: Create your personal brand statement

1. YOU: First assemble all the YOU words. Look at your brand personality and passion words, personal brand adjectives and all the positive attributes you wish to include from having completed your Johari window.
2. DO: Next, identify your DOING words. Write down all the things you do in your job or current role. Even if you are a stay-at-home mum there are still many tasks you do: menu planning, chauffeur, peace keeper – you get the idea! You will have skills and particular roles you're good at. Perhaps you are also an expert organiser, communicator, hair colourist or analyst. Other "doing" or action words could be: organise, mediate, communicate, listen, facilitate…

3. THEM: How do you help other people? You need to identify how what you do has an effect or impact on your clients, customers, employers or those who you serve. This then becomes another set of words.
4. You now work toward a catch phrase or statement by writing out a number of long sentences that sum up YOU, what you DO and how it helps THEM – your target audience.

It will take time for you to condense these sentences down. What you're ultimately seeking is a clear statement that communicates what you in your career or your role stand for and what you offer.

To give you an example of how I would work towards developing my personal brand statement, I would write down a very long-winded sentence like this:

Sue allows her professional brilliance and bright energy to shine through by communication and inspiring results in entrepreneurs and executives to transform, reinvigorate, succeed, bring out their personal best and to shine like stars.

Next I try to condense it down.

For example: *Sue empowers and inspires entrepreneurs and executives to develop their personal brand and shine.*

To condense even further: *Inspiring you to Shine …*

Keep fine-tuning your personal brand statement until you reach that one message that has an impact.

A star is born – Action plan

Complete your Johari window.

Determine your vision and what it is you want to be known for.

Write your personal brand statement.

Two

The Script

"Eighty percent of success is showing up."
– Woody Allen

Years ago, famous producer, actor and impresario, Woody Allen made the statement which is often quoted that eighty percent of success is showing up. Many people have an ambition to become a star, a writer or be a success in their career; however, often it is simply a wish and they don't follow through and do the thing that they want to accomplish. It isn't always the most talented, beautiful or gifted person who succeeds. It is the one who has a go! What is holding you back? Is it fear of failure or fear of success? There's generally something standing in the way. For many people, it is their background story that has either pushed them to succeed or to just accept the status quo and to not bother to attempt anything new or different.

Every good play or movie has a script ... and so does life. There's heroes and villains, tragedy and triumph, romance and heartache. Mix that all together with scenery, costumes, a musical score and action scenes and a wonderful story starts to unfold. The story may just meander along and never really go anywhere. Or it may not excite any audience. Is that your story? Can you rewrite your story and put behind you the tragedy, villains or heartache to emerge triumphant and live the rest of your life fulfilling your potential? Of course, there may be more dramas to unfold – that's just life!

Unlike performing in a play, you do not have to research the background character. By now you will have a fairly good understanding of who that person is as part of your life story has already been written. We have backgrounds to our personal life that often determine our outcome. Many people have a story that they'd rather forget because it has shaped them in such a way that it now seems impossible to overcome. We all make decisions every day and sometimes they are the wrong ones. Nevertheless, we can move forward from whatever happened in our past and forge ahead in a new and more positive direction. As life goes on, there's usually something to deal with – whether it is a major setback such as the loss of a spouse or parent at a young age; overcoming a painful divorce or abusive relationship; or being born with a disfigurement or physical disability. Sometimes it might be something seemingly insignificant at the time (such as a negative comment from a teacher) that holds you back from reaching your true potential. You can change the script. It is not what happens to you, it is what you do about it.

I can only speak from my own experience and share my personal story ...

My story

It was a Saturday morning and I had just flown into Armidale in regional New South Wales. My head was pounding and so was my heart. The head from the massive hangover I had from trying to quash the anxiety and trepidation I felt as a result of many pent-up years; and my heart because I was about to meet the child I'd given up for adoption twenty years before.

We'd spoken on the phone the previous week. It was a call I'd received out of the blue but I'd really been expecting it for twenty years as I always knew deep in my heart and gut that we'd meet again someday. It wasn't a matter of positive thinking or planning; I felt it was just meant to be even though the odds against meeting a child given up for adoption in 1972 were weighted against me.

As a young girl growing up in the suburbs of Brisbane I always had the desire to do more, be more and have more of what was on offer in those times. For me, suburban Brisbane in the 70s was a very boring place to be. I was ambitious and knew that I wanted to live a bigger life. I followed that desire using my main assets at the time: sixteen-year-old good looks and quite a confident personality. I wanted to be a model so I set off on that path by attending a grooming and deportment school and learning all about this life.

I became a model after entering a modelling contest while still at school and winning a modelling course. That set me on the path. My first job out of school was working in a fashion agency as a stenographer and in-house model. I instinctively understood that in order to be successful I would have to become well-known. So, as befitting the times, I proceeded to enter any modelling contest and beauty quest available. Believe me, in the early seventies in Brisbane that was the best way to get noticed. At that time, beauty pageants were a big deal. I was a teenage girl living at home; going to parties; having fun; being feted and photographed, and meeting lots of boys. Sex wasn't talked about then; contraception certainly wasn't discussed and we experimented as most young people do.

In January 1971, I entered another competition and was selected (along with four other girls) to travel to Manila in the Philippines as a "Dial Golden Girl". It was such a big deal for me. I was over the moon with excitement as we were to be there for six weeks, modelling the fashions of Australian designer Paula Stafford and Filipino designer Eddie Ocampo. Dial Soap was famous for putting on fashion extravaganzas; daily choreographed fashion shows held at the rooftop restaurant of the Hilton Hotel in Manila. And we got to live at the hotel in our own room for all of that time. Wow – how thrilling for a suburban Brisbane girl to be living the high life in such an exciting city!

Being the "stars" that we were and all being young, pretty blondes, we soon attracted the advances of the young men about town. And they were impressive; with their fancy cars, wealth and romantic wooing – so unlike any of the local Australian boys we knew. Manila is a city of divided classes: the very rich and the very poor. The young men assigned to look after us and show us the sights were well-educated, well-travelled and had the money to spoil us. Being such impressionable young girls, we soon fell for their charms.

In my case, I was wooed by Eddie who was the son of one of the elite, wealthier families in Manila. He drove a white Stingray Corvette and lived in Bel Air – a private gated community in the Makati district of Manila. It didn't take long for Eddie and me to become an item and spend all of our spare time together. We were young and in love.

The tragedy

Eventually, the day came when we had to return home and go back to our mundane lives. However, Eddie vowed to visit me in Brisbane soon and he did! In the following April, he visited for two weeks. He stayed with my family and me in Brisbane and we did manage to have a weekend or two away on the Gold Coast. A couple of months later, I discovered I was pregnant. Of course, I thought I would get married and go and live in the Philippines; however, Eddie had other ideas and that was the end of that short-lived romance.

As you can imagine, being pregnant with an "Asian" baby in white 1970s Australia didn't go down too well with my parents. I was told to leave home and I did just that; leaving three weeks before my 18th birthday, catching a bus to Sydney and arriving on my girlfriend's family doorstep with my suitcase. My girlfriend Vikki had been one of the girls on the trip to Manila. Her parents were understanding (and probably thankful that it wasn't their daughter) and were happy for me to stay with them for a couple of weeks at the pub they owned in Woolloomooloo.

I soon found a job handing out leaflets for a city restaurant. I also found somewhere to live, at a boarding house in Double Bay. I don't remember having any money and I certainly wasn't given any by my parents. There wasn't any pension for unmarried mothers or anything else like that in those days. But the few dollars I did make covered my living expenses and I occasionally caught up with my girlfriend and my brother who was in Sydney for a coffee or a night out. I was reasonably content; I was just biding my time and, to a certain extent, enjoying the freedom of being a young girl on her own in a big city like Sydney. Once I started to "show", I worked for a family in Vaucluse as their live-in nanny. That was interesting to say the least. It was a case of total exploitation: having to do the cooking, look after four children when they were not at school, and doing "light" housework such as cleaning toilets.

Throughout this period, I had regular check-ups at the hospital and various talks with social workers during which it was always assumed (and encouraged) that my baby would be given up for adoption. Of course, I wanted to keep my child. I daydreamed constantly about how I could go back to work as a model and have my child in day care. Or find a way to return to Manila and make Eddie take responsibility for our baby. Making it a reality just didn't seem possible and with discouragement from every corner and no family support whatsoever, it wasn't discussed. I was in Sydney to have a baby, give it away and that would be that. So that is what ended up happening and I signed the adoption papers.

Towards the end of my pregnancy, I left the Vaucluse family and moved into The Royal Hospital for Women in Paddington where unmarried pregnant girls were kept in a ward of the hospital to await the birth. This was one of the major hospitals arranging adoptions at that time.

On an early morning in January 1972, my baby daughter was born. The first thing I remember seeing was her shock of thick dark hair before they quickly whisked her away from me.

I did get to see my daughter a few times in the maternity ward and I got to hold her; bawling my eyes out every time. It was gut wrenching and heart breaking. There is such an emotional bond and attachment to your child. Knowing that I would never see my baby daughter again was a feeling of such deep sorrow. However, life went on …

This book is not intended to be an autobiography and there have been countless stories of young single mothers and their children who were victims of forced adoption practices that were in place in Australia from the late 1950s to the 1970s.

This practice caused heartache for many young mothers, fathers, families and adoptees growing up. To such an extent that in Australia a national apology was given by former Prime Minister Julia Gillard who stated, "Today, this Parliament, on behalf of the Australian people, takes responsibility and apologises for the policies and practices that forced the separation of mothers from their babies which created a lifelong legacy of pain and suffering."

Suffice to say, overcoming tragedy or heartache of any kind is difficult. But we can and do overcome these sorts of events in our lives, and can go on to rewrite a story that has a happy ending.

Rewrite your script

Your background story is a part of who you are; however, it doesn't have to become your future script. Often people do use their background experiences as an excuse for not pursuing their dreams. Likewise, they may put the blame on others or circumstances for their unhappiness and lack of motivation. And yes, real tragedy can strike anyone. Nevertheless, my hope for you is that whatever curve ball life throws at you, you will stay on course to be the IMPRESS*ario* you choose to be.

But what makes people whose lives have been turned upside down by a freak accident or occurrence keep going? It is recognising the good in simple things – and in life itself.

One lady I know – Ali France – had her life turned upside down by a freak accident. Ali was waiting with her four-year-old son for a lift in a shopping centre carpark when an elderly man lost control of his car, pinning the mother of two's leg between two vehicles. Her left leg was amputated and, after numerous operations, she was unable to walk for two years. However, in late 2013, she found comfort in a new pursuit: outrigger canoeing. According to Ali, who was quoted in a newspaper article, "It's been a long road."

"Canoeing is very therapeutic. It's given me a focus and something to aim for. It focuses your mind more on what you can do instead of what you can't do."

Ali is now an award-winning champion, having won gold in her category at the Outrigger Canoe World Sprint Championships. She said, "I've been training so hard because I wanted to teach my two sons that no matter what happens in life, you've got to pick yourself up and strive to be the best person you can be.

"The last five years have been a real struggle for me and my family and it's only been the last six months that I've felt at ease with my body and my future. This sport has helped me do that.

"When something like (the accident) happens, you want to get back to your old life and it takes a lot to change your mindset. Now I'm happy with my life."

I can't pretend to know what was going on in Ali's mind during the time of her accident and recovery, but I am inspired by her example of thinking no matter what, there is some enjoyment to be found in each day. She re-wrote the script of what her future could be and now has an inspiring story to share.

Even though your IMPRESS*ario* quest may not always go according to plan – or be on schedule – the ability to perform to the best of your ability will mentally drive you forward. There are many motivational books available on the market and how to succeed quotes are coming at us from all angles. Consequently, we can often think there is something wrong if we're having a bad day or that we have to be "motivated" to keep on going. But waiting for motivation doesn't just happen. It literally is about putting one foot in front of the other. Or, as one of my friends whenever she is asked the question, "What are you doing?" replies: "The best I can."

While writing this book, I was reminded of a lovely quote from the late author Dan Poynter who said, "A writer who waits for motivation is a waiter not a writer."

A writer, singer, actor, entrepreneur or you just need to do that one thing and keep on with it. We do get distracted. We bask in small successes or wallow in mistakes that keep us from maintaining focus and commitment and taking the next step. To be a true IMPRESS*ario* and producer of your own success story, remember back to your big picture goal and take those incremental steps to get there.

The triumph

My early "script" did cause heartache, yet I did not allow it to stop me from pursuing my dreams. Early on, I had made up my mind that I would create a successful career. Deep down in my soul I knew that one day my story would have a happy ending. That happy ending came when I met up with my daughter twenty years later.

The day I met Naomi was one filled with such mixed emotions. I was happy, nervous, excited and sad about what had happened, all at the same time. No doubt she was feeling pretty much the same. I remember getting out of the taxi when I arrived at her parent's house and the first glimpse I had was of her peeking out at me from behind the window curtain. I recall being struck straightaway by the family resemblance. She was also a very pretty, young Eurasian girl with long, dark hair. We hugged, started talking, getting to know each other, sharing photos and learning about each other's lives throughout the intervening years. As it turned out, we had started to search for each other when the Adoption Information Act legislation regarding changes to privacy was introduced in 1990. She was living in the USA at that time (where she had lived for most of her life) and began her search when she decided to move back to Australia. It took two years before we did eventually meet up.

For both of us, life during those intervening years has had many ups and downs, twists and turns. After all, that is life. But, fortunately for us, we are now happily reunited. We have also shared many of those life experiences, just like any mother and daughter. We've shared family experiences of marriages and deaths, and the most wonderful of all – the birth of my grandson. We are a family. In a way, it all seems pretty normal to us now; after all, these days families are blended together in all sorts of ways. We will never be able to relive those first twenty years of her life. She did live with another family and grew up in different circumstances with different experiences. We are lucky, yet I know for some people the outcome of adoption hasn't been all smooth sailing.

In 1997, five years after my daughter and I reunited, we travelled to Manila together to meet up with Eddie. I had tracked him down through a mutual acquaintance and sent him a fax! Seems appropriate that I faxed him after he'd f%@ked me! That's my attempt at humour and I don't harbour any hard feelings toward him now. I have chosen to move on from the negative feelings I had toward him and to forgive and forget – although he did attempt to "friend" me on Facebook! Let's just say that I chose to leave that request and that experience in the past.

Part of moving on is letting go. For a long time, I felt shame and guilt and I often wondered, "What if?". I didn't tell anyone about my "secret" because skeletons were kept in the closet. I was a "bad" girl, even though I was seemingly successful, going on to win a major beauty contest; Miss Asia (which coincidentally was held in Manila) and re-establishing a successful modelling career. On the outside I appeared successful, but I believe I suffered from low self-worth. As a result, some of my behaviour after my pregnancy (such as getting involved in party drugs, drinking too much and being in an abusive relationship) was I now believe a subliminal way of punishing myself. Enough with the psychoanalysis already! We all have "stuff" and such is the Australian way of life that we don't really embrace therapy as much as we could or possibly should.

My story is one I have dealt with quite well I think, and these days my life is good and happy. Life will continue to have twists and turns; however, I decided early on that I couldn't continue that way and so I would strive to be the best version of myself I could, despite any setbacks. Holding on to your vision of the future is what can keep you moving forward. Sometimes just trusting your instincts and believing it will all work out in the end … is exactly what happens.

When I was living in my room in that Double Bay boarding house, I had a borrowed record player and had bought one album – Elton John's *Your Song*. I played that vinyl record over and over again, singing along to the meaningful lyrics which seemed to be written just for me and, like any wistful teenager, daydreaming about my future.

Understanding your purpose and objective for this life and nurturing and using your talents are vital for your happiness and success. Can you write the script of your future life story, be the star of your own show and direct your life so that it has the ending you aspire to? There may be a few eruptions, volcanos and villains to come; however, setting the path, leading the charge, and staying on course as much as you can will lead to a more fulfilled career or life destiny.

The script – Action plan

Identify what might be holding you back.

Revisit your big picture vision of what you want to achieve in life.

Write your script for an IMPRESS*ario* life.

Three

Star Quality

"Star quality is one of the most difficult things to describe. It emanates from the person, and he may not even understand it himself. It's a quality that separates the star from the rest of us."

– Richard D. Zanuck

What is it that gives some people star quality? Why is it that some people succeed while others don't live up to their potential? What sets one person apart from others and makes them stand out from a long list of candidates?

The audition process for actors and performers can be gruelling. There are so many people vying for the same role and even well-known superstars will be up against their acting counterparts trying to win a major role. Business owners trying to win clients; job candidates looking for a great role; or even singles in the dating game hoping to meet a partner – everyone in these scenarios faces competition.

If you want to stand out at work, in your business or even in your social life, having appeal and charm will set you apart from the rest of the pack. What is charisma and how do we achieve it? Is it really an elusive concept? Or is it even a characteristic that is necessary for success?

Uncover your charisma

Other words used to describe charm and charisma are personality, appeal, captivation, allure, fascination, having the "X factor" or star power. Wow! That all seems like a tall order and one that us mere mortals can only imagine living up to.

But is it really the case? Perhaps those words are really words that can be used to define someone who is totally confident and comfortable with who they are and not afraid to share it. Some charismatic people can also be totally engaging and fun to be with, but they are not necessarily successful within their careers. So in defining star quality and being a successful IMPRESS*ario* I believe that it is possible to acquire the necessary characteristics to sufficiently captivate people's attention to stand out on your chosen stage. You don't have to be the most remarkable person in the room; you just have to stand out to those who count.

What is success and why is it important? We are all different and have our own unique qualities. In this way, my version of success is no doubt quite different from yours.

Success to me is about realising your true potential – tapping into your unique gifts or talents and sharing these attributes with those who are important to you. It really does come down to your values. One person may need reward and recognition; another may wish to contribute and be of service; yet another will want to succeed to be able to spend more time and experiences with their family. Understanding your values will help you set goals, make plans, utilise your talents and help you aim towards your final objective.

As a teenage girl living in the suburbs of Brisbane, I always had a yearning to be a model or a singer or a TV star. Perhaps it was the influences around me at the time: the fashion magazines I would pore over or the talent quests on TV hosted by young presenters. I did attempt to enter a singing competition at one point until my older brothers laughed their heads off and said, "You can't sing!". So that put an end to that plan.

I hadn't received any singing training and the only experience I had was at home singing along to records with my family as the audience. We were all "enthusiastic" singers but there didn't seem to be any natural talent evident amongst any of us. Families can sometimes be too honest or not supportive enough to believe in your dream. There will always be "dream stealers"; you just have to believe in yourself. I can laugh it off now. Years later, I did do some singing training when I was studying my acting course. After about one year of studying singing and dancing, I decided I was pretty good … and so I auditioned for *The Rocky Horror Show* which was being staged at the Theatre Royal in Sydney.

I'd rehearsed for weeks, learning the words and practising the movements I would act out during my song. Finally, the day came and my jelly-like legs managed to transport me up the stairs and I found myself there on centre stage – in the spotlight. Down in the audience in the darkness were three producers including the legendary Tim Curry, who was famous for his role in the film version as well as the stage show.

It was almost as though everything was happening in slow motion and my brain and body were in different places. My knees were knocking, my palms were sweating, my heart was pounding as I stepped up to the microphone and I started to sing.

My voice was up in my throat somewhere and I couldn't get a note out because I'd totally forgotten to breathe. All I could do was launch into the actions. I turned around, started to undo my dress and act out the part of Janet. After about twenty seconds, a booming voice from the shadows mercifully announced, "Stop!". They then asked me the question, "How much singing experience have you had?" I blubbered something, they blabbed back something about needing good, experienced singers and I couldn't get out of there quick enough. Consequently, I didn't get my chance to shine as a singer and star on stage as Janet in *The Rocky Horror Show*.

Perhaps in those early days, my brothers had been right after all! I do believe that it is possible to learn how to sing and dance and with enough experience become proficient at these skills. Nevertheless, it really is true talent that triumphs overall.

Growing up, I didn't have lessons in any activities such as singing, dancing, tennis, horse riding or any other extra vocational pursuit. We just played, took part in sport at school and occasionally went on beach holidays. It was a very simple existence until I discovered *Honey* – a UK fashion magazine – and my path to becoming a model was set. I did have a belief in myself that modelling was possible. I don't know where that came from as I was a skinny, ordinary kid. Certainly no one suggested it to me or encouraged me in any way other than to simply say: "Do well at school".

I think that most people can probably learn to sing; however, not everyone has the natural talent necessary to take them to the top. Nevertheless, I do think that if we can uncover what our talents and passions are and then learn these skills, with perseverance we can achieve success in our chosen field.

Modelling behaviour

There are leaders in every field and by observing their characteristics and what makes them successful, you can also learn how to apply some of these principles to your own situation. It is not about changing your personality but, rather, about modifying your behaviour. As an example, I read that Richard Branson was extremely nervous onstage when organisations first started inviting him to give talks. However, understanding that in order to get ahead he needed to be able to master communicating and pitching to investors, he persevered and overcame his early shyness.

Fortunately, I did uncover my passion to be a model during my school days. My early influencers were those glamorous girls in the pages of the fashion magazines I would buy. I wanted to have my hair cut like them and wear the same style of clothes. I wanted to believe in myself; that one day it could be me. Of course, genetics did play a part in me travelling that path, yet I certainly didn't have any stand-out qualities that anyone would recognise way back then. I learned how to become a model by going to a modelling and deportment school. I'd saved up enough money to attend the course by working in a fruit shop and then later selling shoes in a department store on Saturdays while I was at school. When I did begin work, I continued to learn from the more experienced girls in the business. By "modelling" the behaviour of the leaders in the field, I soon became sufficiently accomplished to obtain regular work.

Who are the stars in your field? Can you list their star qualities? What are the characteristics and behaviours of these leaders and people you admire? Perhaps one of your influential heroes is an effective communicator and confident networker who makes friends and contacts effortlessly.

But, like the young Richard Branson, not everyone is like that; possibly you just feel totally uncomfortable in these situations. Well, I do have good news for you! You can learn to be socially competent. It might not come easily to you at first, but with time and practise it will. If this is your particular case, it is crucial to read as much as you can about networking and communicating. Go to a few network events with others at first and practise some of the behaviours from the books and articles you've read (including further information contained in this book). It won't happen overnight but it will happen.

I am not saying it is a simple remedy; however, you may surprise yourself by what you can overcome and accomplish. Try something new each month. Make a plan. If we were to use the example, for instance, of networking and public speaking – two important leadership traits – I would suggest the following approach: Month One, learn what you can about networking and attend at least two events. Then in Month Two, attend another two networking events to build on the previous month's experience. Also in this second month take a public speaking course or join a local Toastmasters or similar organisation where you can hone your presentation and public speaking skills and also develop your competency as a networker. Perhaps you are aware that the leaders in your field are excellent sales people or great at social media. Once again, note what those characteristics are and learn what you can by practising a new skill each month.

I once knew a guy who was in his late 40s when he decided he wanted to learn how to ride a horse. He was a roguish character from inner city Melbourne who had lived a colourful life "in the hood" so to speak and was looking for a "tree change". Buying a property and riding a horse seemed to be the right fit for him. Well, he did manage to learn to ride a horse – from a book! I was there the day he first sat on the back of a horse, held on to the pommel for dear life and was led around by another rider holding the bridle.

He later went on to compete very successfully as a Western rider in equestrian events. Horse riding was not his innate gift or talent; however, the yearning to live a country lifestyle, along with a strong desire to stand out (proudly wearing the full Western regalia) and to compete and win, was part of his character.

Learn how to play the part you want to play and to become the leading light in your field.

Let others shine their light

Confident and charismatic people are aware that it is not always all about them. I love the slogan I recently saw on a T-shirt: "Get over your selfie". In today's world where people broadcast just about everything about their lives, it is definitely worth remembering. Make sure that it is also about the fans, your supporters and the people you are dealing with on a day-to-day basis. Successful interpersonal communication is one key to exuding star quality.

As a former public relations professional, I was taught that communication is always a two-way process. It's not just broadcasting your opinions and thoughts but tuning in and listening to others as well. You have to be able to understand what your customers and clients want and need before you can give it to them. Even in daily conversation, be sure to listen to others, ask questions and tune in to who they are and their interests. Others will find you fascinating if you show how fascinated you are with what they have to say. Former US President Bill Clinton was renowned for making people feel special. He would speak to people as if no one else was there, making that individual feel as though they were the most important person in the room. Most personal brand statements about Bill Clinton said he was charismatic.

Heads of State and other charismatic leaders work and play in influential circles. Who is in your circle of influence? The oft repeated expression: "You are the sum of the five people you spend most time with" is attributed to American motivational speaker Jim Rohn. You may think that means hanging out with millionaires if you want to become one. Maybe that's not such a bad idea if that's your goal, but the intent is to be inspired, uplifted and supported by those closest to you. In this day of home-based businesses, many people work independently and only have their family around for support; that's fine as long as you feel nurtured and loved and encouraged by these people. Be mindful of who is in your circle of influence.

Who are the leaders and influencers you admire or feel have star power and allure? Where do they congregate and can you become a member of that network? Join in the community of like-minded, influential people where you know you belong. If you hang out with the "rat pack" or the wrong crowd at school, as Mum used to say, you will end up like them.

Pride, passion, personal best

The notion that we are always on stage when we're out in public or away from the confines of our own lounge room can seem a bit daunting. Uncovering the key to your charisma is to also understand the importance of pride. Displaying an air of confidence when you walk into a room, meeting or any public situation demonstrates a strong sense of self-esteem. You might not always feel like you are the most charismatic person in the room. In fact, you might think, "I'm too short, tall, big, small, unintelligent," and the list goes on … You are you and you have your own set of accomplishments and strengths. Acknowledge that by reminding yourself of past successes and feelings of accomplishment, appreciate the value you bring to others and own your confidence. Easier said than done, I know. I was reminded of that when I worked with a coach who encouraged me to list everything I thought I was good at.

Why don't you try it?

Exercise: What are you good at?

List ten things about you that you consider are pretty cool.
List five compliments that friends, family and colleagues say about you.
What are three things you know you do better than almost anyone else?

In Chapter One I asked you to list down words about your personal brand and characteristics to summarise who you are. However, the exercise you have just done should be a reminder of the value you bring to others and encourage your sense of self-pride.

Captivating people have a zest for life and exude enthusiasm. This passion for what you do, the world around you, and being interested and engaged with other people translates into an upbeat, positive person. Who wants to be around a stick-in-the-mud? Your likeability factor will increase if you are passionate about life. After all, there's lots to appreciate and enthusiasm is contagious. On a number of occasions, I was lucky enough to attend the *Logie Awards*; the big TV "Night of Nights" in Australia. One time I sat with some young personalities who whinged about "having to be here". They demonstrated disdain and a real lack of enthusiasm for the night. Guess where they are now? Yes, that's right – nowhere!

As a publicist, it was my job to look after these TV personalities and be pleasant and easy to get along with. I just needed to take an interest in who they were and be a nice person. That's not always easy when other people don't treat you the same way. Of course, not all stars are disrespectful; it's the ones who really are a pleasure to be around who stand out above the rest. Yes, sometimes we may need to "act" the part of being fascinated and interested in what other people are saying or doing. However, in my opinion, that is one quality that exudes charisma.

Your personal best (or PB) is a benchmark that is usually reserved for athletes when aiming to score a little better each time during training sessions. When developing your "X factor" set high standards for yourself and always be prepared to show your best side. It's how you show up every day that counts. It will also become a habit. Your behaviour and how you interact with people are integrally connected to your reputation and personal brand. You want people talking about you, but you want them talking about you for the right reasons. You might be great at your job; however, if you are painful to deal with no one will like you. Have you had the experience where someone has invited you to join them for a drink after work in order to get to know you and become friends? Or have you ever received a bunch of flowers from an admirer and all of a sudden your interest in them is piqued? Sometimes we just need to know people care about us and like us. Not giving to get something in return, but because we care.

My final key to unlocking your charisma is to care about others. Demonstrating that you like someone else, and having respect for their thoughts and opinions often means that they will like you in return. Having empathy with others and recognising how they may feel requires stepping back and looking at the situation through their eyes; or standing in their shoes to see how it might feel. At a seminar I once attended the speaker got all of us to take off our shoes, place them in front of us and then move one seat to the right. We were then asked to step into the shoes of the other person. Well, it did raise a few laughs, of course – along with a few grumbles and exclamations! Yet, the point of the exercise was that it felt different to be in someone else's shoes; it made us uncomfortable and recognise that sometimes we do need to step outside of our own space to understand another person's feelings.

Star quality is not being false or someone else. It is about being genuine, being you, expressing your individuality and the authentic best possible version of yourself.

Star quality – Action plan

Uncover your strengths to display confidence and charisma.

Learn from and model the behaviour of leaders with star quality.

Have passion for what you do, pride in your ability to do it and give it your personal best effort.

PART TWO

Prepare for the Role

Four

The Rehearsal

"Life is what happens to you while you're busy making other plans ..."

– Allen Saunders

Performing a role or playing your part in the game of life is about making your own luck which, in turn, eventuates as a result of doing the work.

An impresario is someone who directs or produces an opera or theatrical production. You are the impresario of your own life and career since what bigger production could you be involved in? To impress is to make your mark and be noticed; to make an impression.

I don't believe that "impress" is a dirty word although lately I have noticed a trend towards that viewpoint. Some people consider that to impress others is being unauthentic or false, and so perhaps believe this word has negative connotations. This may be due to the fact that sometimes people's behaviour is intended to impress or draw attention to themselves. In the same way that a two-year-old child throws a temper tantrum, it becomes all about me – I want what I want right now! Also it can include teenagers looking flirty and pouty for a selfie image on Facebook. And, yes, we have all heard about famous celebrities who have figure or face-enhancing alterations to increase their power of doing nothing more than impressing for shock value.

For me, the true intention is to stand out and shine to others by being the best version of yourself. Yes – you will impress and have an impact and, as a result, be remembered. It is about enhancing what you have and allowing your true potential and your personality to shine through. Not in a false way to brag or boast and puff up your chest to show off like a peacock. Rather, it involves having the strength, self-esteem and inner conviction that what you have to offer will make its mark.

Actors and performers have to audition for the parts they play and so do we in our lives. In our work or career, in order to get a job we need to impress at an interview or to gain clients, we need to ensure we make an impact at a meeting. We don't just turn up and "wing-it" … or at least we shouldn't. We will have a much better chance of success if we are well-prepared and have rehearsed our role.

Having a positive outcome in our mind before we stand on stage or enter a meeting will certainly help us. Actors, performers and athletes often have rituals to get into a "state" or their "zone" before a performance. As a speaker, I know the importance of thorough preparation, being well rehearsed or having my notes well thought out. Props should be prepared, PowerPoint slides created and many other details ticked off the list before the presentation begins.

However, before that moment arrives it is essential to be willing to find the work and do the preparation. You can't just wait around for that part to come to you. You need to go out and actively seek what you are searching for: the part, the job or the business success you desire.

The audition

For me, having a background in media didn't just happen. In the beginning of my career, there was a certain amount of luck involved. Well, I guess you could call it that; or maybe it was a case of bravado – putting myself up in front of others to be judged in beauty contests. Yes, it does seem archaic now but, at that time, it was one way of getting noticed. From winning beauty contests, my luck kicked in and I was asked to appear on TV in Brisbane, becoming a weather girl on Channel 0-10 for a short time. Then, a year or so later, I heard about auditions being held at Channel Nine and became the weekend weather girl there. That was a great job and I loved learning the role as well as the experience I gained. It wasn't until some years later that I realised that it was a golden opportunity and a potential pathway to a career in television. However, at this point, I had other ambitions and moving to Sydney and pursuing my modelling career was what I had in mind.

Life happened. I did have a long and successful modelling career and it wasn't until many, many years later that I eventually returned to television ... but not without putting in the necessary hard work.

Many of the media greats – whether in television, newspaper or radio – started their careers as young reporters or announcers in some far-flung region and paid their dues working as cadets before hitting "the big time". These days, it seems that you study for a degree and then expect to be given a prime time job. Of course, it can happen that way. However, traditional media opportunities are quite limited now because the whole media landscape has changed and many regional networks broadcast from one central hub or have fallen by the wayside to become digital only. Nevertheless, making the effort to study a degree, acquire the knowledge and gain the experience (either in a regional or metropolitan area) will ensure you are well-grounded for a future in media if that is your chosen career path.

Although I wasn't young when I returned to television, I was prepared to change and be flexible – all essential attributes to achieving your dream at any age.

After studying acting for three years and as a long-term relationship was ending, I took the plunge and moved to Wagga Wagga, a regional city in the Riverina area of New South Wales as the News Anchor for Prime Television. I don't think I would have gained that job without studying and honing my skills as an actor, doing voice training and applying for at least a dozen other presenter roles. Of course, being prepared to move to a regional city (where I knew no-one) certainly went in my favour.

At a couple of those auditions, even though I did not get the job, I was given the audition footage; this helped me win the Prime TV role. Learning on the job was the best experience of all. Not only about learning news reporting from senior, well-seasoned journalists (who had a fairly narrow view of a blonde, former model reading the news) but also learning how to work with a team to produce a successful outcome. I did not have a degree, nor had I studied any form of media. Instead, I worked hard, gave it my best shot and was able to use the experience I gained as a stepping-stone to another television experience.

When Prime Television was expanding, I applied for a role within the network in Wollongong. I was knocked back the first time, but I persisted and did get selected as a weekend news presenter and public relations manager, which was a newly created role. Again, lacking any formal communications or public relations experience or training, I learned on the job. I ended up staying with Prime TV for another three years.

Following my time at Prime TV, I went to several other auditions for jobs, received a few knock-backs and then eventually moved to ABC Television in Sydney as a senior publicist. I stayed there for six years, working on a range of documentaries, dramas and entertainment shows where I arranged publicity for the personalities, programs, and their producers. I spent ten years in broadcasting altogether and loved it – but as I have already mentioned, none of it just landed in my lap.

If you truly believe that the role you desire is destined for you and your self-belief is strong, you will do the hard yards to turn your dream into a reality. The question is: how do we gain that conviction and self-belief?

Belief – you have to want it. You need a strong desire; call it lust or love. It's that feeling you have when you are engaged with something you truly love doing. Above all, you need the courage to go after your dreams. How many times have you thought: "Oh, it would be nice to …". I know I certainly have thought like that in the past and then not followed through.

We've all heard the stories of people who take off for a year or two; pack up the kids in the car, sell all their belongings and travel around the country or overseas to have a life-changing experience. That takes courage. I've often thought: "Oh, wouldn't it be nice to live in a foreign country for a year or two; learn the language and immerse myself in that culture." But I haven't done so up until this point because the desire has not been strong enough to take me there. It is a "nice to have", not a "need to have". Other goals and ambitions or dreams have taken priority in my life.

In this way, you need to believe you are capable and deserving enough, plus have a virtually burning desire which is related to understanding why you want to achieve a particular outcome.

Why you, why now, why not?

Discovering your why and understanding your purpose in life has recently become a mantra and the subject of many books, coaching programs and the like. Even though it will help you to uncover this information, sometimes you just don't know what your true purpose is. Furthermore, your purpose might change over time. Perhaps you're young and carefree and your current "Why?" is to make a living so you can travel, see the world, have freedom and meet lots of new people. Or maybe you're just married and your purpose is to have a successful business, buy a house, put down roots and gain some future security. Or maybe you're recently divorced, still young and carefree and your "Why?" is to make a living so you can travel like you did once before, see the world, have freedom and meet lots of new people.

Awareness needs to come first of what it is that you want. It's similar to an actor becoming aware of a role. The next step is to understand what the role involves and having the capability to perform it. Then there is the audition – trying out for the part – after having first undertaken the research and being prepared to do your best.

What is it that you want? It's a big question and often the hardest one to answer. While it can take a while to work it out, it shouldn't stop you from starting to achieve your dreams right now. Often people wander around aimlessly not knowing what it is they want. Or they stay in jobs they don't like because of the security, not knowing or trusting themselves to try other options. They are in a state of confusion or, even worse, inertia.

You might select a goal and focus your energy on it, but if you don't put enough concentrated focus into turning that goal into a reality it is a waste of time. We might set a goal that is too unrealistic as our major end point without breaking it up into smaller goals that are possible to achieve first. For instance, you might decide you want to be the CEO of your own million dollar business. Not unachievable, but it most likely won't happen in your first year of business. Don't give up; set yourself a realistic goal. It could be to achieve a turnover of $100,000 in your first year and a smaller target of $10,000 a month. What sales do you need to accomplish in that month to reach your target? Work this out and stay laser focused on making those sales so you reach your goal. Sounds simple, huh? Of course not! That is why there are so many goal setting and success strategy books and courses available and people go from one to the other seeking the ultimate answer.

It is also that self-belief, worthiness, headspace "stuff" that holds us back and gets in the way. Do you make up reasons why things won't work out rather than why they will? I don't think I am good enough to ... or I can't afford it, I really need to stay in my secure job or environment. I'm too old to do it now. My partner wouldn't approve or want me to pursue my dream; it might mean that we end up breaking up. Most of the time these are just excuses. With some planning and preparation and perhaps a heart-to-heart conversation with your loved ones, you can achieve your goals. You will never know unless you give it a go!

I've "ummed and ahhed", procrastinated, had moments of self-doubt and fear about being exposed before I started writing this book. It has taken quite a long time for me to get to the place where I've thought: "If I don't do this now, I never will". That would mean that I'd not have shared my story and experiences with people I could potentially inspire or help in some way.

If you've read this far, thank you! I think by now you get my drift; for lots of reasons we put off doing something we really want to do. If you're going to succeed and be an IMPRESS*ario* you'll need to prepare, motivate yourself, and ask for what you want. Preparation comes with doing the pre-work and having some sense of absolute willingness or confidence to start. For some people, it comes with planning step-by-step whereas, for others, it is a matter of having a broad outline and just getting started.

Motivating yourself could involve visualisation and meditation, or coaching to support your vision. I don't believe in, "I'm waiting until I'm motivated" or "I'm just not motivated right now". Sometimes we expect "Motivation" to be like taking a pill; once you've got it or had a dose of it everything will be fine. However, like having a headache or a sore tooth, you can't ignore it – you have to do something about it. Sometimes we've just got to get going and do something about it; go to work and do the job. Self-motivation is just doing it – take the action and push through until you reach your goal.

Asking for what you want is all about visualisation and putting your dream out into the universe – attracting the success you desire. Now we all know it is not that simple, but there is evidence to support the concept that desire + action = a great result.

So read those books, do the courses, meditate, visualise, get the information, but do the work as well. Do whatever it takes to become the IMPRESS*ario* of your life.

I will summarise what I have learned or read about goal setting in the section below.

Goal setting

FANTASY + FOCUS + FOOTWORK = FAME

Your goals should be aligned to your values. By understanding and articulating those values and motivators, you will be able to achieve the outcomes you want. You've already done some work in identifying your values when you worked on your personal brand identity. So let's revisit those concepts again …

Often people want fame and recognition; the most common aspirations for people are to be wealthier, happier, healthier, wiser, more appealing, and more powerful. But when you break it down what does being wealthier really mean to you? Is it to be a millionaire? Perhaps it's to have sufficient income for a fabulous home and overseas holiday every year? Does being wealthier mean freedom to you or security or accomplishment?

What do you fancy and perhaps dream of and fantasise about? It doesn't have to be some huge, lofty ambition such as being famous and winning an Academy Award. (Or it could be!) Perhaps it could be to win a major business women's award in your community to gain recognition and ultimate growth for your business. What is meaningful to you? Having a good reason behind your goal – your "why" – does help you to retain focus. Why do you want to make one million dollars?

Another aspect to goal setting is to review all areas of your life. Being an IMPRESS*ario* is about designing the life you want. If your business and career is going fantastically well but your personal life and having enough time for friends or romance is a problem, those concerns are the ones you need to address. It isn't necessarily about work/life balance as you may be currently completely driven to achieve your major career goal. But do examine all these areas to understand what you really want. So get busy and write down what you want to achieve in each of these six areas:

1. Business/Career
2. Financial
3. Home
4. Personal/Spiritual
5. Health and fitness
6. Family and friends.

What does success look like to you? As I write this, I have a photocopy of a cheque that I received from Amazon for a small royalty amount from the sales of my first book. It has the amount scratched out and replaced with a much, much larger figure. It is on my vision board, along with a number of other images and each day as I meditate I bring that image to mind. It is a fantasy at the moment but with visualisation it might happen. Follow me on social media and I'll let you know whether or not it comes true!

Exercise: Create a vision board

Visualisation is a powerful technique. For this reason, I suggest you create your own vision board to picture in your mind's eye exactly what you want to achieve. I had a vision board posted up on the back door of my bedroom in a previous home. I'd look at it each day; I can still see some of those images in my mind now, but I can also see them in reality. I live in a house with lots of windows and light and it is by the water. In the grassy backyard with tropical trees, there is a small table and two chairs – just like the picture I cut out and pasted on the board all those years ago.

Create your vision board by cutting out images and words from magazines that represent your goals; what you want your impressive life to look like. Choose images that are representative of all six areas. Personal life might mean exotic travel or caravanning with kids. Home could be a simple cottage by the water or a palatial mansion. This is your fantasy so choose images that are meaningful to you. Take your time to enjoy this process. Make sure you have a large variety of magazines from different genres and put on some soothing music to put you in a peaceful mood. Let your intuition guide you to your images.

Get a large-sized piece of cardboard and start pasting on images and words to create a collage. I also like to frame mine. You can pick up something from a charity store and replace the painting or photo with your vision. Place your vision board in a spot where you will see it each day. Another idea is to photograph it and keep as a screensaver on your phone or even on your computer – it's up to you. But have it where you will be reminded of your vision often.

Fantasy to focus

To turn your fantasy or your vision into what it is you want to achieve requires tremendous focus. Focus is easier said than done when there are so many distractions in life. (Oh! I just got pinged!) In theory, you already know that you should stop doing those things that won't bring you closer to your vision and start taking action on the tasks that will get you to your desired result. Having a vision board is a wonderful reminder that we should try to break down some of those desires into a to-do list (i.e. set some achievable goals). Concentrating on doing one thing at a time and ticking that off the list does create momentum and helps retain the necessary focus required to push through.

Backward planning and small steps will help you reach your goals. Articulating and putting a timeframe on each step will help you get to where you want to go. You probably know this already yet most people don't take the time required to write out their goals. Take one major goal at a time. To use writing a book as an example (and ultimately receiving a big cheque from Amazon!), I need to start somewhere. In this case, a written, clearly articulated goal might be to have 20,000 words written in two months. Let's say we put a month on it; by December. How would you break that down? Writing 10,000 words a month means 2,500 words a week. Realistically, it might not happen because other activities – work and life – get in the way. Sure I'd rather be sitting with the girls after yoga having coffee; however, if I don't go home and write at least 1,000 words I won't achieve my goal this week and another week, month, year will have gone by. Is that what happens to you? Do write down your goals and chip away at them by having focus and taking action. If your goal is to be a millionaire, are you just visualising and wishing and hoping? Or have you found a way to earn an extra $20,000 by taking a part-time job and putting it toward a deposit on an investment of some kind? Do the work, find out what it takes to become a millionaire, a writer, an actor or IMPRESS*ario* in your world and focus on achieving your clearly defined goals.

Footwork

Oh, yes, this is the hard bit. Actually going for that run in order to become healthy. Picking up the phone to set a meeting with a prospective client. Find a way to do what you need to do. Alternatively, of course, you could be thinking you're taking action by writing yet another business plan, reading, researching, being busy doing what? We all do things that waste time and don't get us closer to the mark. It's not easy. Right this second, while I'm writing these words I'm distracted and thinking of the phone calls I should have made this week. There's always so much to do in life so take it one step at a time.

Exercise: Create your action plan

I find the best way to take action to achieve the incremental steps on the way to the "bigger picture" goals is to formulate an action plan. Put a timeline into place. This could be a spreadsheet, a project management system, a document with columns and rows, or simply a notebook with your goals and action steps written down. Your WIP – or work in progress – needs to have an end date to it, with the smaller action steps that need to be accomplished on your way to achieving your big goal. Let's say you have set your sights on becoming an accomplished keynote speaker. What would you need to do to achieve this goal? Some of the tasks would be to write a speech; design a presentation; get some speaking coaching; get some voice coaching; practise your speech; rehearse your speech in front of an audience and contact organisations who would be interested in your presentation. There would be a number of steps involved in your goal. Determine what they are, put them in order and put a timeframe on them. Each time you complete one task, move on to the next. Step by step you will have done the footwork to turn your fantasy into your version of fame.

To make your own luck – work for it

Sometimes I think life is just one big audition. All of us are to a certain extent "waiting in the wings" for our moment to step into the spotlight. You might be in the spotlight now: a leading business person or a famous singer. You might have made a success of your career and be perfectly content with your place in the world right now. If that scenario applies to you though, there still might be other less lofty ambitions. That's the beauty of life – to have hope and to move forward with some purpose.

As an IMPRESS*ario* the easy part is to research your role and write your script. The hard part is the commitment to turning up every day ready to rehearse, practise, face your fears and audition to bring that script to life.

You are an IMPRESS*ario*; this is your life to live so be sure that you make your own luck.

The rehearsal – Action plan

Create a vision board of what you want to achieve.

Actively seek out the role you want and prepare for your success in that part.

Set goals, focus and do the footwork to turn your fantasy into reality.

Five

The Costumes

"Clothes Maketh the Man."

– Shakespeare

In the play, *The Tragedy of Hamlet, Prince of Denmark*, costume plays a major part. The Prince wears an "inky coat" which signifies he is mourning for his dead father. Yet, Hamlet doesn't feel that this outward sign – his "suits of solemn black" – can even begin to express his grief and anguish. He is the only one in court still wearing black; it sets him apart from the other characters who have taken to wearing bright colourful clothes to celebrate a new King and an exuberant court. This deliberate choice of costume tells us something about the inner character of this man.

Costume has been part of theatre, film and stage for eons. The visual spectacle of seeing beautiful or striking costumes, without even feeling the fabrics or wearing them ourselves, arouses our senses. The visual image adds to the impact of the character and aids the storytelling process. For example, witnessing a character in rags who becomes a refined lady, such as Eliza Doolittle in *My Fair Lady*. Likewise, Jaime Lannister, a character in the television series *Game of Thrones*, who at one stage appears as a prisoner – downtrodden with dirty hair and tattered clothes – but who, later in the series, resumes his true role: wearing regal armour as a knight of the Kingsguard. His change of costume paints a contrasting picture to his initial persona.

What sort of image do you want to portray? You can use costumes to enhance your own personal brand and style, and paint a picture of the person you want others to see you as. Now, that may seem frivolous or inconsequential; however, what I'm referring to is making the most of what you have. Presenting your personal best and putting a shine on the best version of you.

Before we don a costume though, we need to first do some basic work– on our foundation. Now, I don't mean your body; we all come in varying shapes and sizes. What I am referring to is working with the basic "you"; the image and innate qualities you already have.

Accomplishing the brand image and style you want to project to the world requires a bit of forward thought and planning. By now you will have the framework of your brand identity written down. Who you are innately and what the future potential you want to step into is like. You have described that person. So how would that character appear? Is it as a sophisticated, professional with a creative edge? Perhaps it's a bright, modern-looking CEO or a casual, yet glamorous work-from-home entrepreneur. Remember, this is your story – paint the picture of the costume your leading character is wearing.

A picture tells a thousand words

Iris Apfel is an American fashion icon and celebrity who is ninety-six years young. Her flamboyant style is what is most memorable about her; the unique way she wears colour, as well as her outlandish glasses and various pieces of jewellery.

A friend of mine is also a very colourful personality. She always wears beaded necklaces, bright clothing and accessories. She is a diminutive woman, but you certainly wouldn't miss her in a crowd! Her style is unique and makes a statement. Neither of these two women embodies my style aspirations, yet I admire the way they express their personality and personal brand through what they wear. In the male department, movie star, Johnny Depp wears his brand of smart casual, albeit slightly grunge and eccentric. While David Beckham's sartorial choice is a slim fitting, sharp suit.

In the case of my friend, her choice of career over the years has not been conventional. Corporate style is not something she has ever considered or been drawn to. Iris Apfel worked in interior design – a fashion-related business where creativity and style is revered. You may not necessarily aspire to be avant-garde; however, you can develop a signature style that helps you feel comfortable and confident with what you're wearing and express the best version of you.

Let's examine a couple of airline brands and the "look" they project to the world through the attire of their staff. For example, Virgin Australia has a strong corporate image of being friendly, fresh and cheeky. On the other hand, Qantas has an image that is far more conservative and corporate-looking. Both companies spend millions of dollars on getting their "look" right and reinforcing a strong brand message. Not just the external branding of logos and signage, but also the uniforms and image of the people within the organisation.

At a business seminar I attended, one of the speakers – a well-known successful businessman – wore a well-tailored suit, crisp white shirt with French cuffs, expensive cufflinks and smart tie. He looked the part of a very successful businessman. The other speaker, who was equally successful, worked in the organic food industry. He also looked sharp, yet he wore fashionable, casual linen pants and blazer. Both men were well dressed and very reflective of their respective roles and professional brand image.

By understanding the brand qualities you want to project with the work you do and in alignment with the clients you work with, you can create a "look" that is suitable, creative and stylish to help make your mark.

Regardless of whether you work in a corporate environment or as an independent entrepreneur, as an IMPRESS*ario*, YOU are the package. What does your "package" look like? What is your design, colour and signature look? What message does your personal image send? Your clothes and appearance are part of the external image of your brand. It's not only your logo that needs to look good as being representative of your brand – so do you!

Exercise: Create your visual image

In order to "up the ante" and express more of who you are through what you wear, the following suggestions will help you to create an image that has an impact on others.

To begin this process, work with the words and adjectives you've identified via your Johari window of the type of person or brand you would like to project. Think of yourself as the product you are designing a package for. Create a brand portfolio of ideas and visual examples by cutting out images from magazines and producing a scrapbook, or

---

search online and make a Pinterest board of your favourite styles. Find looks and colours that appeal to you and that you believe are the visual expression you want for your self-brand. Take stock of whatever appeals to you visually. Fashion and costume designers often have a "look book" or a cork board that has pieces of fabric, sketches and other ideas in their line of sight to provide creative inspiration.

Determine who your business style or fashion icons are. Is it glamorous Cate Blanchett, suave Daniel Craig as James Bond, or the bohemian fashion look of Rachael Zoe? Or maybe you aspire to a rock star look. Collect images of these people and see what the common thread is. Is it the simplicity of style, the colour choices, the cut and fit of the garments? Add these to your file of the fashion looks that appeal to you.

What colours appeal to you? Your colour choices may say more about your style than you may realise. I love the colour gold. Here's a summary of the information I read about gold on several colour psychology websites.

Gold represents loyalty and responsibility. It is also seen as the colour of success, achievement and triumph. When your primary choice is for gold, the colour personality tests consider you an organiser. You love a peaceful environment, you value work and service oriented tasks. Gold is associated with abundance, quality and prestige.

This description may be only one aspect of my personality, but when mixed with other colours I like, I have a more holistic understanding of my personality characteristics. Try it yourself to see what your favourite colours say about you.

What objects and things do you love? Are they treasured pieces of fine bone china or bold brass statues? Does a particular style of artwork stimulate you? Write down or collect images of objects that appeal to you.

Do you have a favourite or ideal holiday destination? How would you describe that and what does it look like? What does your ideal home look like? Once again, thinking about that visual representation will give you more insight into your style influences.

Once you have noted all these visual elements, you will see some common threads emerging and you can then start to determine your signature style. For instance, are your images, cool, white, Scandinavian and simple clothing styles. Or maybe they are colourful and tropical?

From this overall visual impression, you can start to break down into detail your personal image management plan. This can involve styling yourself using clothing, to the supporting look you can achieve via hairstyling, accessories, makeup for women, and the finer details of presenting your personal brand package.

Be your own stylist

I worked with one client on his personal brand who loved the colour black. This colour symbolises authority and power. It is also considered to be a formal and prestigious colour; representing sophistication and a sense of mystery. When combined with other objects and elements he liked, the brand persona we eventually arrived at was functional, stand apart and power. When developing his signature style, we wanted him to look powerful and streamlined with modern, simple straight lines in his black suits and other items of clothing. However, we didn't want him to seem aloof or unapproachable. Consequently, the brand look and photos we orchestrated had him appearing with contrasting lighter shirts and a warm smile.

The style images you have collected may be flamboyant or perhaps seem unrealistic for you to attain and wear in your industry. However, consider these images as being a reflection of just a part of you, or perhaps the creative edge to be explored a little further. Maybe it is not always possible to express exactly what you would like. I think Iris Apfel would raise a few eyebrows if she was advising clients in a law firm, or seeing patients in a health clinic. But wearing her fabulous trademark glasses might be enough to give her personal brand that stylish edge, especially in her chosen field of interior design.

Step into your personal power. Consider yourself as a brand and IMPRESS*ario* by choosing to wear what suits and enhances your character and reflects your personal brand. Personal branding should support who you are. Whether that brand may at times need to stand out and be different, or dress to be part of a team or tribe, successful brands have personality.

Let me tell you about Beverley's story (not her real name). Beverly was a mature, extremely accomplished leader who worked in an educational institution. She excelled in her job; however, the management board thought that her "look" was letting her down. Why did this even matter if she was great at her work and no one questioned that? It was due to the brand positioning of the school and the target market they wanted to attract. Beverley was seen as being the figurehead, but also as somewhat dowager and old-fashioned, who lacked rapport and appeal to progressive, modern students; and to the parents who were making the education choices. In fact, Beverly had just remained in a rut and was dressing in the same way she had done for years; never considering that it might have a negative impact on her career.

I see this scenario regularly; where people have purchased a few expensive suits and then they wear them over and over again. Guys are guilty of this too. For example, some men will wear front pleated pants and a boxy jacket which makes them seem old-fashioned and dated.

In Beverley's case, she was open to change. Rather than considering it to be a personal affront, she welcomed my advice on how to update her look. She loved going on a shopping trip and having a new hairstyle, and felt renewed as a result. When I followed up with her some weeks later, Beverley reported that she felt a stronger connection to her market.

Every so often it pays to review your "look" through fresh eyes. You can seek advice from a trusted advisor, friend or shop assistant or consider a do-it-yourself make-over.

Exercise: Create your personal brand look

1. Complete your research to create your personal brand "look book" of clothes, hairstyles and shoes – inspirational looks and colours that appeal to you. Don't think about the prices, what should be work outfits or play outfits, or where to buy these items. Just collect examples at this stage and soon a pattern will emerge. This is the foundation for your brand style.

2. Review your own wardrobe first. The idea is to cull down to only what works for you and start to build on that foundation. Try everything on. If it doesn't fit or is tatty, get rid of it. If the colour doesn't work with your complexion, get rid of it. Using your inspiration board, look at what's left. Are there outfits that you can compile straightaway?

Once you've sorted through your wardrobe, can you determine if you have a certain look, a set of colours, or a signature item that could set you apart?

There are well-known speakers who use colour as their trademark. Helen Macdonald from The Corporate Optimist always wears orange. Naomi Simson, CEO of online business RedBalloon always wears red.

3. Put together a shopping list of several items that will work with what you have already and a wish list of a few items or outfits that will help make your "look" go from good to great.

You may only need a few quality signature pieces that you can mix and match, and that reflect your individual style. You don't have to look different every day; you just need to look good, appropriate for the occasion and make an impression. I know a number of women who work in the fitness industry; these days, because activewear is so fashionable, you would never see them in the oversized T-shirt and daggy leggings of old. They mix and match their activewear outfits and impress wherever they go.

With the rise of online fashion bloggers, you will see so many examples of people who have crafted a brand identity around the way they look.

A speaker I know reflects her "Let's Grow" philosophy by always wearing a flower on her lapel or floral skirts and outfits. Another person always wears sparkles. Customise your costume to ensure you stand out.

4. When it's time to hit the shops, you don't have to spend a lot of money. You can just add in a few new pieces to give your wardrobe some life and reflect your personality. Think of your wardrobe as a growing, evolving adjunct

to your personal brand and not a static object without any life. If you shop wisely, and only buy the things that you love and that reflect who you are, you will develop an impressive wardrobe over time.

6. Sort through your wardrobe each season. Replace any basics that are starting to need an update or smartening up. Then you may only need to buy one or two pieces; an accessory or a couple of really great outfits that have impact. Guys can follow this example also by regularly updating their shirts and trousers, and occasionally a new suit or jacket.

5. Plan your outfits. I've done my own version of wardrobe planning for years so maybe you can adapt it for yourself. When I worked as a television news presenter, I was lucky enough to be able to borrow clothes to wear on air. I'd write down in my diary what I wore each night and then the following week I'd borrow different things. I'd also note what each outfit looked like on camera, and if it didn't look right, or the colour didn't suit me, I wouldn't repeat that outfit. I'd even take note of the comments other people made about my appearance. Rightly or wrongly, someone always had an opinion!

On the following page is an example of my seasonal wardrobe plan based on the colours I wear most: red, black, white and beige/tans, plus the occasional blue/navy tones. I do wear other colours depending on the occasion, my mood and to liven things up every so often. I haven't included jewellery in this list; however, each day I'll add a couple of pieces from my collection. They could be classic pieces or perhaps a state-ment necklace, earrings or bracelet. This is your basic everyday working wardrobe plan. I do wear other "costumes" on occa-sion, particularly if I am speaking or presenting on camera.

My Spring Wardrobe Plan – Southern Hemisphere (September, October, November)

Day	Outfit	Accessories
Monday	Navy skirt, beige shirt	Nude-coloured ankle boots and nude-coloured bag
Tuesday	Red wrap dress	Red and black shoes, black bag
Wednesday	Black dress, Beige jacket	Black high heels and bag
Thursday	Floral skirt, Red jacket	Black high fronted shoes and bag
Friday	Business casual outfit: Black pants and black button shirt	Black kitten heel shoes and bag
Saturday		
Sunday		
Monday	Lace skirt, Black shirt	Black ankle boots and bag
Tuesday	Blue dress	Black high heels and bag
Wednesday	Brown skirt, Beige jacket	Nude-coloured ankle boots/shoes and nude-coloured bag
Thursday	Black business suit and multi-striped shirt	Black ankle boots and bag
Friday	Business casual outfit: Camel pants, White T-shirt, Beige Blazer	Nude-coloured ankle boots/shoes and nude-coloured bag

Saturday		
Sunday		
Monday	Black and Yellow dress, black jacket	Black high heels and bag
Tuesday	Black business suit pants, beige jacket	Black ankle boots and bag
Wednesday	Black bow skirt, Black lacey top	Black high fronted shoes and bag
Thursday	Red and black dress	Black high heels and bag
Friday	Business casual outfit: Black jeans, white shirt	Black ankle boots and bag
Saturday		
Sunday		

I rotate these three weeks' worth of outfits, four times over. Following this wardrobe plan for twelve weeks will mean that you only wear that one outfit four times during the season. Mix and match and you can create numerous styles.

There are now apps available on the market you can use to upload images of all your clothes, shoes and accessories, plus inspirational "looks" to create your own online wardrobe. A couple of apps I have tried include Stylebook and ClosetSpace. Or simply use an Excel spreadsheet like the example given above or online tools such as Evernote or Google Keep.

"I have nothing to wear"

All this planning might seem too controlled for you and make your head spin. After all, shouldn't fashion, costume and style be about creativity? Yes, of course, you can be spontaneous, go out and buy that fabulous outfit. Don't take the fun out of fashion and shopping. But, here's the thing. So many people (and women in particular) have hang-ups about clothes and shopping.

Let's now consider a few different scenarios:

- I am too fat. I'll wait until I lose weight. I am too tall (or short) so nothing I buy ever fits me properly.
- I can't afford to buy what I like.
- I have a wardrobe full of clothes but can't manage to put anything together or find anything I really like.
- I hate walking into a shopping centre/department store/boutique as I get confused. I can't find anything and the salesperson is either too pushy or can't be found.
- I've tried online shopping but had to return everything because it didn't fit properly.

Have you ever used one or more of these excuses to avoid looking and feeling your best? I know I have in the past, particularly the one about "money and affordability". I grew up getting excited about a new box of hand-me-down clothes arriving from my cousins and feeling sad about not being able to have a new party dress because we couldn't afford it. I still find it hard to go out and have a big "splurge" buying clothes or max out my credit card. And that's not necessarily a bad thing. With wise wardrobe planning and shopping, you can still look great without over-extending your budget.

Most of these excuses we come up with are self-esteem issues. "Stuff" we've grown up with or acquired over the years. Like a number of other key areas in IMPRESS*ario*, we may need to examine these excuses in more detail to figure out why we feel this way and look at measures to address our self-esteem issues.

Let's knock a few of these issues on their head right now!

Money: If you don't invest in yourself then who will? As I say in my workshops: the GFC (Global Financial Crisis) is over. Now GFC means, "Good For Your Career". With some planning and budgeting, you CAN put a stylish wardrobe together. We invest in learning new skills for our careers, paying our mortgages, going on holiday, kid's education and the like. Why not invest in yourself? After all, you are worth it. Even if you are starting out and don't have a lot of money to spend at least invest in some items; one or two outfits to wear to meetings and networking events that make you look exquisitely YOU and exactly the way you want to appear.

The amount you spend on clothes is up to you; however, decide on a portion of your earnings that you can set aside. Whether it is 5%, 10% or whatever – plan your wardrobe budget and only buy what works well and looks fabulous.

Costumes for an IMPRESS*ario* are "tools of the trade". They are a personal "overhead cost", but essential investment in dressing to stand out.

Physique: Don't underestimate the value of a well-fitting outfit. No matter what size you are, you will probably own a few outfits that do fit well and look good. Shop for those brands as it is likely they will continue to provide styles that fit and work for you. If you can't find a perfect fit but you've found something that is close, have the garment altered to fit. With the trend today toward online shopping, often the fit of a garment is not as good as it could be. So be willing to go through a bit of trial and error to determine the brands that suit you best. Buy things that may be slightly bigger on you and have them altered so that they fit properly.

Retail therapy: Shopping can be fun and window shopping for ideas and inspiration can be entertaining. However, when it becomes a case of, "I've bought another black jacket to go with the four other black jackets I already have" it could be a problem for you. The solution is to avoid shopping on impulse, or when you feel bored or a bit down and you're looking for a quick pick-me-up. Think it through and try to resist the urge. It's a bit like having that extra piece of cake – you know you really want it but you also know it is not the best decision. Go back to the original plan. Does this garment really work with other items in my wardrobe? Do I really love it? If it is a one-off piece, will it be something I will be able to wear on another occasion?

Feeling overwhelmed: Sometimes it may seem all too hard to buy clothes and so you end up with nothing. This scenario is the exact opposite of retail therapy. It's very frustrating because you spend hours at the shopping centre and come home empty handed. Or worse, you get there and don't even bother; you just don't have the confidence to pick out something and try it on. You've succumbed to that defeatist attitude of "nothing looks good on me." Take a few deep breaths, set a goal in mind and take a shopping list with you. Perhaps your list will simply be one dress or shirt.

Start off small and aim to accomplish purchasing that one item that looks great. Take it home, try it on again and see how it works with other items in your wardrobe. A lot of stores will give you a refund if you change your mind. If you are really hesitant about shopping, make sure that you shop in those stores first so if the item just does not look right when you get home, you can always take it back. Next time, make it two items and slowly you will build on your shopping successes and establish a great wardrobe.

Invest in yourself by working with an image consultant who will help you with many of these issues. They are trained to assess your body shape and will discuss your personal brand and assist you to choose colours and styles that will flatter you. Yes, it is an outlay initially; however, it is definitely worth the investment if you want to take that next step: to being a true IMPRESS*ario*.

There is nothing wrong with spoiling yourself and feeling uplifted from the powerful feeling of looking your best. As one of my clients said, "What your consultant did for me in the clothing area has paid BIG dividends in my life and is continuing to impress."

Pay attention to personal presentation

Up until this point, we've been considering the "nuts and bolts" of wardrobe planning. Now let's consider some areas where we've "shopped til we've dropped" and we have the great wardrobe, but it still doesn't look right. Perhaps it looks great in your eyes but others might not agree with you. Is your look appropriate? This is such a minefield I know and none of us want to be told what to wear by some superior being. But hopefully we have enough self-awareness to consider what will express and enhance us, yet still be appropriate and impress our audience. "Dress to impress" is an expression that has been bandied around for years. Is it still relevant for the 21st century? Yes!

Of course, we can still wear our shorts, PJs and old clothes at home if we want to. But turning up at work in what you'd wear running around on weekends or out to a nightclub is not a good idea. I have seen women turn up at work in a corporate environment wearing very short shorts. Okay, maybe she had great legs, but what do you think people were saying about her behind her back that day? Or the executive who works out at lunch time and doesn't bother to shower or change out of his or her exercise clothes for the remainder of the day. Looking like you "don't care" may reflect your attitude to your work and possibly diminish your credibility.

Even models and actors who are in a sense a "blank canvas" for the director or photographer will make an effort to standout and be noticed during the audition process. It may be through adopting a significant style of their own, or perhaps dressing the part of the character they are hoping to portray. It is intentional influence.

You might work in a situation or reflect a fabulously creative vibe where everyone is super casual. And, of course, there are a lot of hugely successful companies where productivity and brand is not influenced at all by what employees are wearing. Yet you would find that the heads of these types of businesses would still dress professionally (maybe even in suits) if they were meeting with bankers or investors. Likewise, if you are an accountant or lawyer, you would not be frowned upon for looking more businesslike and dressing like the professional they expect to see. Even Mark Zuckerberg (of Facebook fame) ditched the hoodie and wore a suit when he got married out of respect for his bride and guests.

Creativity is the key and I encourage you to explore it. It is simply that it is not sloppy. Put some thought and intention into your dressing style. As an IMPRESS*ario,* you are your own brand and your outer visual package should display that in a fabulously flattering way.

It is also worth investing in your personal presentation and grooming; it doesn't need to be hard to maintain. A great haircut, manicured nails and a healthy appearance with clear skin and eyes should be the norm.

For women, makeup is a personal choice. I know some women choose not to wear any makeup. Personally, I like the made-up look but I'm aware that it should not be too heavy, especially in business meetings. However, I would advise you to wear makeup if you are presenting on camera or in front of people. It will give you a bit of colour and "warm" you up a bit. Get some expert advice on this if you're not used to wearing makeup.

Men should be clean shaven or have a neatly trimmed beard and moustache. The hipster look is hot at the moment and can look great if it is maintained well. Your best accessory is still your smile – but don't forget the shoes! Clean shoes and no downtrodden heels. Generally, women don't have a problem with this because we love shoes! Guys sometimes just don't think about it. My husband used to work in retail and often men would come in to the shop to buy a new suit. He would always ask them if they needed such accessories as a tie, belt or shoes to go with their purchase. Adding a new pair of shoes was often thought of as an unnecessary expense. So his reply was, "Would you buy a new Porsche and put re-treads on it?"

Most of this is common sense; however, in my extensive experience working in personal branding and corporate image consulting I've seen many cases where it's not common practice. I always remark, "You are a walking, talking business card for your brand and business." What sort of impact do you want to make through your brand image?

Professional portrait to portray persona

An initial first impression is often made online these days and as an IMPRESS*ario* and representative of brand "You", you need to ensure your visual appearance supports you in communicating your brand essence. Apart from style and the clothes you choose to wear, your profile photograph is very important. You should definitely have one and ensure that it is a professionally photographed image.

Recruiters, potential clients, customers, colleagues and competitors are viewing your social media pages on a daily basis. Therefore, it makes good sense to present the best version of you visually, as well as through interesting, engaging summaries of who you are, what you do and insight into your interests and ideas.

The first step in preparing for your personal branding photo shoot is to consider what image you want to portray through all of your marketing materials, including your photo. If you are in business, no doubt you have considered your logo, fonts, colours, wording and other elements of your brand collateral. But whether it is for a business or personal outcome, you should carefully consider the "look" you want to portray to others. Are you now better able to understand and capture your essence?

Your core personal brand essence should be now well-defined as a result of undertaking your personal brand audit. You understand how you want to be perceived and what you want to be remembered for. Consider the ethos of you and your business or work, and the description you came up with. Do you want to be seen as fun loving, a high-achiever, friendly, formal, professional or creative? What sort of photograph would help support your traits and what you stand for?

Think of yourself as the product you are designing a package for. Remember the image styling exercise you did when coming up with your visual brand representation. Cut out and collect words, images and colours from magazines. Select images of clothes and shapes that appeal to you and reflect the words you have chosen for yourself. As you undertake this exercise, you will begin to discover your style and what appeals to you. Also look at the images of executive portraits or business owner photos to see if there are looks that you like. Observe the poses, backgrounds, colours, props and other elements that make up the photo. Cut out some of these images and create a brand portfolio of ideas and visual examples. Take this with you to the photo shoot so both you and the photographer has an impression of the style you are aiming for.

Dressing for photos is "occasion" dressing – just like attending a job interview. You want to reflect the best image of yourself and to be appropriate for the occasion. Do your research. You wouldn't go to a client meeting or job interview without knowing something about the company. Think about what your clients or potential employers are looking for. If you work in finance, law or other professional services, they want you to look like a credible, successful businessperson. Alternatively, you might work in IT or a creative field. Your potential client wouldn't expect to see you in a three-piece suit. However, does that mean you need to wear a sloppy polo shirt or low-cut evening dress? You want to make a good impression and that won't happen if you dress inappropriately.

As a rule, if you work in a creative industry, you should aim to look creative. If your industry is more conservative, portray that style. As I work with a lot of senior executives (mainly in a corporate environment), I do wear a slightly more classic look; however, I like to add a creative and modern edge to that. A classic, conservative look doesn't mean old-fashioned; keep current and up-to-date with the latest trends.

Consider your personal brand style or a signature look or accessory. Previously, I mentioned a speaker colleague who always wears a large flower on her jacket lapel or may wear a floral dress or skirt. It is a reflection of her brand name and "gardening" philosophy. The Australian Master Chef judge Matt Preston is known for his numerous cravats and flamboyant suits of many colours. Fashion designer Alex Perry always wears his trademark sunglasses on his head.

High-contrasting clothing colours, such as a white shirt with a dark suit jacket, work well in photos as they tend to provide a stronger, more defined look. Greys and blues are more traditional colour choices but can be complemented by accessorising with a different colour. For example, grey can look great with orange or green and dark blue; or try teaming it with aqua or purple. Monochromatic colours (i.e. all one shade) portray a more personable image, but they can look boring unless there is a contrasting element such as a statement necklace or interesting neckline. Experiment and try a variety of choices to see what suits you and works well together.

For men, ensure your shirt collar is sharp and sits well with or without a tie. Both men and women need to ensure that jackets don't have "puffy" shoulders which can occur if the jacket is a bit too big, hasn't been pressed well or is a cheap make.

Prepare for your photo shoot by putting a few outfits together at home that reflect your personality, but are also smart and professional. Try them on to see how they make you feel. You want to really like what you're wearing and be comfortable so you feel great and will portray that confident side of your personality. Generally speaking, you will find you have something available in your wardrobe already. You don't have to go out and buy a whole new outfit. Just make sure your clothes fit well, and are cleaned and pressed ready for your photo shoot. Take them into the studio on hangers, along with your portfolio of "looks", and then you are "ready to roll".

For women, hair and makeup are part of the overall impression. A bit of powder will soften any shine and lipstick will brighten you up. Get your makeup expertly done if you haven't got a clue – even if the "natural" look is more your style. Men should focus on smart grooming as well.

Your expression and smile are your most important accessories! Look through the lens of the camera and think of a really happy moment in your life. Your warm expression and natural smile will shine through.

With a little forethought and planning, you can portray the image that suits you best and that sends the message you want.

The costumes – Action plan

Create a "look book" to paint the picture of how you – the leading character – is costumed.

Plan, curate and shop wisely so your wardrobe evolves as an adjunct to your personal brand.

Express your brand "look" through captivating photographic images.

Six

The Production

"If no producer, no movie."
– Dino De Laurentiis

You are the star of your own show; turning up every day to deliver your well-rehearsed lines to bring your ultimate story to life. In this production, you are everything: the producer, the writer, the director, the costume designer, the art director and creator of the vision. As the producer and IMPRESS*ario*, it is you who starts out with an idea for an impressive life and then makes it a reality. That is your role.

The major Hollywood film productions are based on a talented group of people coming together for a short time; bringing their expertise to a project and then moving on to the next production. Witness the rolling list of credits the next time you watch a movie. The actors' names are top of the bill and are then followed by many others in supporting roles. These people are just as important to the overall production: directors, writers, cameramen, photographers, sound and lighting technicians, musicians, wardrobe and makeup stylists, art directors, location scouts, stunt people, publicists, financial controllers, and the list goes on. Overseeing all these elements is the producer who has a team working with him or her to make sure the movie is filmed, edited, marketed and distributed to major cinemas worldwide. The producer makes the film happen. And you can also make things happen by enlisting the help of others to bring your production to life.

Who's on your team to help you stage the play of your life? Bringing your production to reality takes more than just wishing and hoping. It does take a lot of planning, determined effort and plenty of help and assistance along the way. As much as we like to think we can "do it all" ourselves, having a support team around you to prop you up in the beginning and to rally around when it's time to launch into the "big time" is an essential part of being an IMPRESS*ario*.

Create your success team

Who is on your team? And who can you enlist either for the short-term or long-term?

Some roles to consider in terms of people who should be on your team to help you become the star you're destined to be are outlined below.

An Agent: Not perhaps in the literal sense of a theatrical agent – though I did have representation when I was acting and when I was modelling. Agents are specialists in their field and have the necessary contacts to help you find work. They recognise and understand what you are suited for, and charge a percentage of your earnings to support their role … and they are well worth it. Other types of agents or agencies could include recruitment, influencer agencies and talent management companies.

A Coach or Mentor: Equally important to guide and keep you on track to achieve your dreams. The coaching industry has really come of age recently, with a range of very qualified and accredited people to choose from to help you reach your goals. Do your research and find someone who has a track record of success with clients similar to you. You'll want to work with someone who can stretch you and who you can be open and honest with. They should be able to keep you accountable to tasks and to drive you to achieve a successful outcome. They don't have to be your best friend, but having a good rapport with them will help. Over the years, I have had mentors and coaches and find that as I progress through my life, I have sought to work with different coaches to achieve a particular target (e.g. a life coach for general goal setting, or a business coach or writing coach).

A group coaching or training program with other people can also be beneficial. It often leads to a small breakaway group or a one-to-one buddy system where you discuss some of your ideas and plans.

Mentoring can either be a formal or more informal relationship where you have someone – ideally in your field such as a boss or manager – who you meet up with regularly for general discussion, guidance and insight into the mores of that role. Whatever you choose, having someone on your team to talk to when the going gets tough – and it inevitably will – is essential.

An Assistant: While watching old movies you would have seen the secretary running after the star to answer every whim and request. You may recall in the movie *The Devil Wears Prada* how Anne Hathaway played the character of Andrea Sachs, the hapless assistant to almighty fashion magazine editor, Miranda Priestly (played by Meryl Streep). I don't expect you to act the part of Ms Priestly; however, having someone to help you with certain tasks while you aim for the top is very beneficial. Your assistant could simply be a cleaner who comes to your place once a fortnight to help with housework and enables you to free up your time for learning or applying your new-found skills to your craft or business. An assistant might be a virtual office assistant, who can help with social media posts to help grow your profile.

Speaking of social media posts, your team could include a publicist. We'll talk more about this role in later chapters where we consider marketing in more detail.

A Stylist: Your stylist might be an image consultant, who helps you create an individual style and coordinate a wardrobe of clothes to suit your lifestyle and look. They will give you advice on clothing colour choices, accessories and outfits to suit your shape so you always look your best.

A Personal Fitness Trainer: This role could involve someone who works out an exercise and diet regime for you so your body is also healthy and performing at its personal best.

Yes, I know you're probably thinking, "I can't afford all this." Maybe all this is not for you right now and you'd have to be a true superstar to live this well-supported lifestyle. But just consider where you might be able to get some support so you can devote your time and energy to the production of your future life. You want to be in a position where you don't get caught up in menial, time-wasting activities that don't do anything to support your dreams.

Personal trainer not for you? What about taking up walking, running or yoga to keep physically fit? Stylist too extravagant? Devour books and magazines on style and image to determine what is going to be the right "look" for you. Go shopping and try on lots of clothes, even if you aren't intending to buy anything. You will start to discover your sense of style, colour and what looks great on you. When you do decide you need to make-over your wardrobe, shop wisely and only buy the right "look" for you. Refresh your memory about how to be your own stylist and create your own signature IMPRESS*ario* "brand look" by re-reading Chapter Five.

An actor might have a voice coach, singing coach or acting coach. They have a team of other actors or friends (mentors) they can call on to run lines or rehearse with them before an audition. Successful actors understand the importance of preparation and having the right team to help them to fine-tune – not just their role but their instrument which is themselves.

When I moved to a new state, I had to find a new hairdresser and other service providers. It took a few visits to different ones before I could find my right team to support me. I collected the business cards of my "suppliers" and keep them together in a stylish business card holder. This is my group of personal service providers and includes my doctor, dentist, massage therapist, physiotherapist, naturopath, hairdresser, beautician and others. I also have a support team for my business: an accountant, lawyer, graphic designer, virtual assistant and support staff when needed. This is not the complete list and, indeed, it might seem rather comprehensive to you. If you were a major corporation you would have a team of directors, managers and staff across many divisions. As the producer of your story, you will also need a support team.

One vivid memory I have is seeing the crew of a well-known motivational speaker, all wearing emblazoned T-shirts featuring their boss, checking in at the airport. At the time I thought, "How fantastic!" Of course, this person needed a large entourage supporting them as they are a big business organisation. But what really stood out to me was the branding. You wouldn't think twice if it was a football team. Seeing the branded collective crew certainly made an impression.

Exercise: Discover your support crew

Review the following list of people you might need on your team to start to identify the perfect crew for you.

Agent
Business coach
Life coach
Mentor
Cleaner
Stylist
Image consultant
Personal trainer
Yoga instructor
Hairdresser
Doctor
Dentist
Massage therapist
Physiotherapist

Naturopath
Beautician
Accountant
Lawyer
Personal assistant
Social media assistant
Publicist

Special event management

Have you ever thrown a party? I'm sure you have. Some parties will have been more extravagant than others, depending on your budget at the time. Think of all the elements you had to bring together: the invitations, the venue, the food, decorations, music and, of course, the right people. You invited people to attend, emailing and phoning them, and pulling everything together; being the event planner. Did your thoughtful planning, coordination and hard work pay off? Did you feel a great sense of accomplishment and end up having heaps of fun? Even if there were a few bumps along the way, I'm sure it all turned out well in the end. Your life as an IMPRESS*ario* is the biggest party you will ever produce ... and it will be fantastic!

As the planner and producer of your life, you get to decide what scenes need to be cut from the show. What isn't working needs to go. However much you might like to think that scene can be tweaked, or played again with a different leading man, sometimes the show will work better without it. You also decide where the true talent lies and what should be nurtured. You also may need to let go of certain people on your support team: those who don't share your vision of who you are and what you can achieve. This doesn't mean that you need to remove these people completely out of your life. But you need to carefully consider what role they do really play.

It is not always easy juggling the demands of home life, family life and work life and the lines do cross over when you are an IMPRESS*ario*. I find the best way is to discuss your plans with those people in your inner circle on a regular basis – perhaps quarterly or monthly. Let them know what is on your calendar, understand what is on their schedule and talk about the expectations about who does what in order to fulfil all the relevant obligations.

Who do people want to work with?

Producers do have to work with difficult people. Or do they? In your production, up to a certain point, you can choose who you will work with. There may be difficult people, clients, customers and encounters to deal with; however, you do have one choice – to ensure that you're not difficult or hard to work with.

In theatre, there is a saying, "There are no small roles, only small actors". Basically this means you need to walk before you run and not let your ego or sense of self-importance – or even frustration – get in the way. As an actor, Marlon Brando was well-known for mesmerising audiences with his very small screen and stage roles when he first began his acting career. It is up to you to be good to work with and do the best job you can, no matter what role you're playing.

Working as a publicist in television and the entertainment industry gave me an insight into how stars are made. You certainly did see big stars with lots of ego succeed purely because of their talent. However, the hard-working regulars also came out on top.

I know who I would rather work with … and it is not the well-known comedienne who feigned hiding under the desk, giggling and saying in a baby voice, "Oh no, the publicist is here. Don't let her see me." Being featured in a magazine was important to her career but she didn't want to do the work. Or the newsreader we all hid from when he visited the publicity department (okay, so we were being childish on that occasion!).

Let me tell you about the "Silver Fox". This particular newsreader was celebrating a milestone; the anniversary of his many years involvement anchoring the news. He was a very distinguished-looking man. He always wore tailored, sharp suits and crisp white shirts. And he had this shock of white hair, hence his nickname the "Silver Fox". In my role as publicist for the news division, I was involved in organising a celebratory lunch to mark his important milestone. It was a catered three-course lunch to be held in the executive boardroom at ABC Studios in Sydney. In order to compile the guest list of VIPs and media, I had a meeting with the Head of TV news to update him on what was happening with the event. I also asked him if he would like to be the one to make the celebratory speech. He turned to me and said, "I won't be there. You'll be bloody lucky to get anyone to attend; the man is a pig, was a pig and always will be a pig!"

As you can see this "gentleman" (to use the word loosely) was not well liked but somehow he did manage to have a long career.

Perhaps your production is still at the early stages; you're leading up to the time when you're producing and playing your part in a much bigger production. Now is the time to continue with the small roles, fine-tune your skills before you reach the accolades you deserve and begin to establish your support team.

The production – Action plan

Your role as producer is to understand and coordinate many elements to bring your story to life.

Enlist others and create a success team to realise your production.

Be the type of person others want to work with.

PART THREE

Showtime

Seven

Marketing You

"Without promotion, something terrible happens.
Nothing!"

– P.T. Barnum

Hollywood spends millions of dollars annually on marketing movies. A sizeable part of any creative production is the money spent on the promotion and publicity for a movie, play or album. Much planning and strategising is required for an audience to be aware of any product. To create a celebrity following and audience for you – the product – involves being seen, being heard and being known. How are you going to achieve that?

A self-marketing campaign, if implemented with intent, will help you – the individual and IMPRESS*ario* – to become top of mind with your audience.

If you are a business owner, there may be several marketing and communication strategies you can explore such as advertising, sponsorships, staging of special events and promotional campaigns. This is in addition to the three main personal public relations areas of networking, social media and publicity that we will be concentrating on in these next chapters.

Before we can promote ourselves effectively, we first need to understand why we want to do so and have the confidence to "put ourselves out there". It does take a bit of bravado to be able to self-promote. However, with a strong belief in your abilities and a good understanding of your "big picture" reason for being an IMPRESS*ario*, you can tap into self-marketing activities to help you to succeed in your chosen field.

It is not always the people who are best at a particular skill or profession who have the greatest success. Often it is those individuals who become well-known and put themselves "out there". Competition is present in every field. On one occasion, I was selected to speak at an event … but only after the organiser had attended another event where another speaker who addresses similar topics to me was presenting. This person is a well-known personality who has done an amazing job of self-promotion; plus he is good at what he does. However, for this event, I was selected based on my depth of knowledge and experience in the media – the subject at hand. The point I'm making here is that my competitor still gets plenty of work because of his high profile and I applaud him for that. A true IMPRESS*ario* is someone who is not only good at what they do but is also known for it. It is also not worth over-analysing the competition: there really is enough to go around for everybody.

My story is one that I haven't shared publicly until this point. My personal journey is one of appearing to possess outside confidence and bravado but actually lacking a strong sense of self-esteem to really believe in myself. This is often referred to as "the imposter syndrome". It equates to having a sense of "I'm not good enough"; feeling shame or thinking "I shouldn't be the one chosen for that particular project because there are others who are better than me". Or maybe you feel very nervous in a particular situation and think, "I've bluffed my way through but they will now find out that I am not competent". Of course, if you are nervous and uncomfortable it means you don't present well so your self-belief ends up perpetuating your own myth. I know I am not alone in this. I've read stories about famous singers and actors who still wonder why they are so successful as they feel as though they are imposters.

Part of my journey and reason for writing this book is to support women by encouraging them to have a strong dose of healthy self-esteem. It is okay to really believe in yourself and your abilities, and to also have the confidence to say no to what isn't right for you.

Networking to make your name in your social scene

Networking is an all-important self-marketing tactic. It requires confidence and being seen at the right events for you and your topic of interest and expertise. It is also beneficial to your profile if you are photographed at these events and these images are published online or in social pages. However, the true value of networking is in making meaningful connections.

Walking into a room full of strangers or people you barely know can definitely be intimidating. But we need to communicate with people in person and have those real face-to-face conversations in order to build strong and effective relationships. It is that "real" contact with others that will help you not only build a network, but gain confidence to converse effectively and have fun at business networking events.

I have a contact in Hong Kong; we met at an industry association event some time ago. I first saw him standing on his own and I took the initiative to start chatting with him as he clearly was a newcomer to the networking event. I had been to the same event a few times previously, knew other people there and didn't feel as uncomfortable as he appeared to be. We headed to the bar, ordered a drink and started to talk about what made him come along and what he was hoping to gain from the evening. I introduced him to one or two other people and then we went our separate ways. Over the years, we've bumped into each other at different business events; we're connected on social media and I know he appreciated that warm welcome as he has told me so. We're not close friends but I now know someone who I can look up if ever I am in Hong Kong.

Over the years, I have attended many women's business networking events and have found that quite often you do seem to meet the same people. Now you might be thinking that's a waste of time; that seeing the same faces and connections will never lead to anything. But for me the opposite is actually the case. I have met many amazing women, have formed strong friendships, and have hired other people and been hired myself through these contacts.

The point is that it's not always about gaining work or business or "doing the deal"; it's about creating real life connections. I'm sure that you already understand the concept: "People want to do business with people they know, like and trust". The best way to gain that trust is to get to know people and build those connections via communication. So let's get talking and mingling at events.

The most important point about attending networking functions is that you're there to meet people and to form effective contacts. You won't do that if you spend your time flitting around the room from person to person or only speak to people you already know. It's better to meet two or three people and have an enjoyable conversation than attempting to speak to thirty people. Focus on the quality of the contact rather than quantity.

There are different types of networking events, including breakfast events, lunches, evening cocktail events and all day conferences. Some of these events will feature a guest speaker or speakers and often some sort of attendee participation is encouraged.

Feeling daunted about the prospect of having to participate? I've attended events where the MC has asked each person in the room to say their name, what they do and perhaps some other piece of information about themselves. At other events, all the people at the one table will be asked to discuss a particular topic or share information about themselves with those in the group. If you're feeling squeamish about the prospect of having to talk about yourself in a room full of strangers, trust me when I say it does become easier over time.

For those of you who feel uncomfortable about this scenario, do your research beforehand to understand what is expected at the event and then prepare yourself. By that I don't mean – don't go. Putting yourself outside your comfort zone those first few times will eventually lead to less nervousness, and a sense of accomplishment and confidence.

When you feel at ease in a networking situation, you will naturally make more meaningful connections with the people you meet and be remembered more positively. Over time, as a result of relaxed communication and building trust, a stranger at an event may eventually turn into a prospect and ultimately a client.

What do you do?

To prepare for your first event ensure that you have rehearsed your "patter". Be prepared for the inevitable question: "So what do you do?" Be succinct and to the point with your response so the other person has a clear understanding of what you do. They may ask follow up questions, so be prepared to talk a little about yourself. However, as soon as you can, start to turn the conversation around to the other person by asking them questions. Once the topic of work comes up, question them about what they do.

The key to building relationships is to listen twice as much as we speak. A networking function can be enjoyable and less confronting if you remember it's also about the other person. Try to make the other person feel comfortable and enjoy being in your company by having a quality conversation. People love talking about themselves and they appreciate others who give them that opportunity. Most people will think you're a brilliant conversationalist if you let them do most of the talking! So how do you do that? By asking questions and engaging in conversation without sounding like an investigative journalist. You'll be amazed at what you can learn that way.

If you do all the talking, how can you possibly build a relationship? Keep quiet about yourself and get the people you meet to talk. This can be quite challenging for a lot of us. I'm still learning to do this myself! On one occasion, I was at a dinner with a new group of people and I was feeling a little nervous. So I kept on talking, talking, filling the gaps, until the point where the person I was bombarding the most who happened to be a very outspoken fellow said, "I can't keep up. You keep finishing my sentences." I'd annoyed him and, of course, what I should have been doing at the time was listening to others as well. As a result, I missed out on the opportunity to build a relationship. It should have been about conversation – not just chat, chat, chat on my part.

As I mentioned previously, the question: "What do you do?" will inevitably come up. I try not to start off the conversation that way; however, if people ask me, then I have my "PBS" ready. In case you're wondering what this stands for – it's my Personal Brand Statement. You should have already fine-tuned your PBS after having read and undertaken the exercise in Chapter One.

You don't want your elevator pitch or ten second commercial "sound bite" to sound a bit "tacky" and false. It defeats the purpose of having a relaxed conversation and getting to know someone. On the other hand, you don't want to waft on incoherently. Keep it brief, clear and memorable.

Next time you are asked about what you do try this approach:

Your name … what you do … who with … what impact it has on them. You should aim to say this in about seven seconds and make it memorable.

For example: *"Sue Currie, I'm the owner of Shine Academy. I help business leaders and entrepreneurs create a brand that has impact and influence, so they shine."*

People may ask me how I do that which then opens up the conversation to further dialogue.

Before you go to a networking event you need to figure out your goal for attending; what is your objective. As an IMPRESS*ario,* your objective might be to connect with someone influential to help you get to the next phase of your profession or to make contact with a potential client. Alternatively, it could simply be to make connections to add to your database.

When starting out with networking it may help you to have a contact or friend who is already familiar with that particular network; someone who can introduce you to other people. If you don't know anyone, the organiser is usually a good starting point. After all, they are there to help people connect with other people. You can simply approach the organiser, introduce yourself and say, "I am new here today. Is there anyone you can introduce me to?"

Following up afterwards is important. Always thank the organiser if they have introduced you to anyone new and send a card, note or email to say how much you enjoyed the event (or the food or the speaker). Keep in touch. If you receive a business card, follow up with a LinkedIn invitation.

In the spotlight

While you are at the event, you could also arrange to take a photo of you with either the organiser or speaker or with a friend and then publish it on social media using the appropriate tags to help showcase the event and yourself. Networking should be enjoyable. It is not about being manipulative but can be useful if you also help promote the event through your social media channels.

If you are not on the so-called "A list" don't expect to be photographed by the media or promoters. There are ways to optimise your chance of being photographed and, over time, that may help you become well-known and perhaps be invited to social events in the future. Being photographed means being in the right place at the right time. Arrive at a time when the photographers are duly snapping away the people coming through the door. Even arrive a little early and mingle outside the event before the doors open if this is suggested on the invitation or program. For example, if the invitation states 5.15 for 5.30 pm start, then arrive at 5.15 pm. It is not about going up to the photographer and asking to be photographed. You want to be known as someone with style, grace and good manners so being blatant is not the way to go. However, if you have been photographed before it is fine to thank the photographer for the previous occasion and speak to him or her as well. There is nothing wrong with networking with them, but do remember they are there to work also.

To be memorable at an event and optimise your chance of being photographed, you also need to look fabulous and stand out from the crowd. Stay true to your signature style but, if you can, accent your style with either colour or a signature piece such as an amazing necklace, scarf or an eye-catching hat. In a sea of dark suits, a "pop" of colour in a blazer or top can work well. It will also capture the photographer's eye as they are attuned to visual images. Colour against dark business suits will stand out very clearly.

Visual images are the ones that stay in our mind. For this reason, it is no accident that Instagram has taken off so well. Newspapers have relied on this concept for years. Having a captivating photograph on the front page (and often back page) of a newspaper is mandatory to capture readers' attention.

Networking action plan

Going to every event in town is not a good investment of your time. These days, you need to be strategic about your networking, depending on what you are hoping to achieve. It is not always about winning clients; perhaps you are new to a city and just want to make friends with like-minded people. This is a great objective. Friends lead to other contacts and eventually – you never know – you may be introduced to a prospective client. None of us have an infinite amount of time so being clear about what you want to achieve is essential. I had a client who was very purposeful about expanding his well-established business in a new city. His networking plan was to commute from interstate to attend his industry events in the new city. Of course, he was aware that there would be numerous competitors; however, he also could rely on friends and contacts he had made over the years to reach potential new clients.

Networking is about building a network of people. It involves getting to know people and understanding each other's needs so you can help each other. Networking is not just about external networks either. Within your organisation, it should be possible to go and talk to somebody face-to-face instead of sending emails all the time. Spend ten minutes chatting to someone in the staff canteen rather than reading your iPhone. Strike up a conversation – simply ask people how they are or what they did on the weekend. Where did you go on your holiday? Did you see that football game on the weekend?

Can you find other ways to communicate and meet with your network? Perhaps you can arrange to have a conversation over lunch or a coffee catch up each week. Coffee conversations can lead to great connections.

Exercise: Become more confident with networking

Why network?

Your reason for networking may be that you want to make meaningful connections with the people you meet and build trust so a new contact may eventually become a client and supporter.

Record your objective and why is it important to you.

What is your resistance to networking?

You may have numerous reasons. However, I think the main reason that people avoid networking is generally due to lack of confidence. To help you to overcome any resistance to networking and give yourself a confidence boost, remind yourself of your contribution to the world by noting your accomplishments and interests.

My passions and special interests.

My life experience, wisdom and networks.

Current and past jobs.

Understand the traits of successful networkers

Name three good networkers you are aware of.

Describe the characteristics and traits of these good networkers.

Preparation

Practise – "What do you do?"

Conversation starters

One of the biggest stumbling blocks to networking successfully involves knowing the best way to start a conversation. A few suggestions include: sport (often a great conversation starter!). Even if neither you or the people you are talking to are interested in football or golf, it may lead to a conversation about what you are interested in. If you've done some prior research you can discuss a topical or newsworthy item. Also try to establish something in common between you and the person you are speaking to that is not necessarily related to your business. For example, you may have both been to the same holiday destination.

Some other ideas to break the ice and begin a conversation are:

- What is the most interesting project you are working on at the moment?
- Tell me about your business.
- What line of work are you in?
- What do you do?
- How long have you been in that role?
- Where are you based?
- How did you get started in business?
- Do you have expansion plans for your business?
- Trends in the industry – what impact do you think XYZ will have?
- Do you find it difficult to find the right staff/contractors?
- How long have you been living and working in City/Suburb/Country?
- Can you recommend any restaurants/places to see?
- What do you do in your spare time?
- Where did you get those fabulous shoes/necklace?

Open-ended questions are best, such as who, what, where and when?

As an example:

- What brings you along to XYZ event – are you a member?

- I'm looking forward to hearing what XYZ speaker has to say. Have you heard them speak before?
- Weather – although not exactly exciting can still be a conversation opener.

It is important to remember that your woes, worries and weight are not the best conversation starters.

Exercise: Determine conversation starters based on these topics

Food
Location
Crowd
News
Books
Films
TV
Write down your top conversation starters to build rapport.
What?
Who?
When?
Where?

Exercise: Networking strategic plan

The first step is to identify who is in your current internal network or circle of influence. How can you connect with the key people or those who would have potential contact with your ideal target in the next three months?

Identify several key players in your potential network.

- How well are you connected to these people?
- Within your current networks, who has the strongest link to these people?
- Who are your current clients and supporters that you have built rapport with? How can you connect, refer business to or network with these contacts in the next three months?
- Who are they connected to? For example, boards, politics, industry bodies, community networks etc.
- Who can they connect you with?
- Who can you connect them with?

Where to network?

Based on the information mentioned above, research the top five network events in your area that the people you hope to meet are likely to attend. Plan to attend each event at least once to determine the right fit for you. Choose two or three to attend on a regular basis.

Over the next six to twelve months, aim to take a strategic approach to your networking to build contacts, create awareness of you and your brand, and potentially create interest in your business or career. One way to do that is to decide on a target, such as a number of meetings generated from attending events or another outcome that is significant for you, and then measure it.

Decide who you will follow up with and how by developing a system, such as inviting them to connect with you on LinkedIn or perhaps meet for coffee. Do try to keep in contact on a regular basis. When you meet someone and exchange business cards, ask their permission to add them to your email list or database. Don't just add them anyway as it's rude and can be considered as spamming them. The last thing you want to do is alienate someone.

Finally, evaluate and measure what has worked, what you could do more of and what you would do differently.

Networking tips

Now that you know the value you bring to a networking event, have planned your conversation starters and have an action plan in place, here is a quick summary of top twelve tips for effective networking.

1. Networking is about making contacts. Five to seven minutes is an ideal amount of time to spend with anyone. Aim to circulate rather than blending in.

2. Set an objective before attending an event (i.e. meet the speaker, meet new people and have three quality conversations).

3. Listen twice as much as talk. People love to talk about themselves, and they appreciate others who give them that opportunity.

4. Don't make a sales pitch at a networking function. You're there to just connect and build trust.

5. Don't pass out business cards to anyone and every-one you meet. Wait until the end of the conversation, when you've established a reason to make further contact, before exchanging cards.

6. Take the focus off yourself at networking func-tions. Act like a host and make other people feel comfortable.

7. Walk into a networking event confidently.

8. Don't head directly to the bar or food and park your-self there. You're not there for the food.

9. Observe where the circle of influence is and mingle in that area.

10. Place your name tag on your right shoulder. As you shake hands, the other person's eye will automatically go there.

11. When it is time to move on, remember to close a conversation.

12. Where appropriate, indicate that you intend to make contact again within a few days. e.g. I'd like to discuss that further, give you a call, will send you a LinkedIn invitation.

Marketing you – Action plan

Understand you add value to others through your unique skills, talents and past experiences.

Plan and practise answering, "So what do you do?"

Create a strategic networking action plan.

Eight

Publicist to the Star

"Early to bed, early to rise, work like hell and advertise!"

– Ted Turner

I do love the quote accredited to American businessman and founder of the Cable News Network, Ted Turner: "Early to bed, early to rise, work like hell and advertise!" However, I like to paraphrase it and use the word – publicise!

Publicity involves free "word of mouth" advertising that comes from mainstream media coverage, such as news stories, feature articles, editorials and reviews, plus radio talk show interviews and television appearances. It is a very effective way to gain attention for you or your business, and is often considered to have more credibility than paid advertising.

Publicity is one function of public relations and sometimes is bundled up under the "umbrella" of marketing. As previously mentioned in Chapter Seven, there are a variety of tactics incorporated in a comprehensive marketing or PR campaign. However, publicity and social media coverage gained through the extremely influential vehicle of media can really catapult you to stardom.

Create your own publicity

The media landscape has changed dramatically over recent years, yet major magazine and newspaper coverage, as well as television and radio are still some of the most effective ways of reaching a wide audience. There are countless online publications and just about all the major media outlets have an online presence.

You've got to wonder how they all survive ... and not all of them do. The successful media outlets have a variety of content to fill their pages and programs. Guess where they get that content? From you. Most of the articles you read that are not major news-breaking stories are ones that have been suggested by a publicist or public relations agency. As you are now your own publicist, you need to make sure you contact the media anytime something interesting happens in your business world. They could come across you by accident or by doing their own research. Large media organisations do employ researchers to keep their finger on the pulse of new ideas and trending stories. But why not be a lot more proactive and get in touch with media outlets via a phone call, email or media release? They need your information just as much as you need them.

At this point you may be thinking: "Well, that applies to big businesses only". While it is vital for businesses, it's also relevant for an individual who wants to make a name for themselves. Plenty of famous personal brands started out gaining publicity via articles, books and stunts. Richard Branson is a master when it comes to staging an event that captures media attention. Even at the beginning of his career, he was in contact with mainstream media.

There are several ways for you to gain media attention. These include being seen at social events as previously mentioned and also appearing in the social pages, or writing a book which you can then leverage to get publicity in the media. This is a good hook and a reason for the media to publicise you. Likewise, writing articles on your area of expertise and being published in magazines on or off line are good options. Appearing on television is the ultimate publicity tool and will fast-track your path to personal brand attention. These are major ways of getting "out there" and making a name for yourself.

Free media exposure has far more credibility than advertising. People are more likely to take notice of something they've read or seen on TV that looks like a story or editorial rather than an advertisement. Having mainstream media exposure also increases your chances of being found via digital media as the large news and media companies distribute content across all these channels. These multi-million-dollar companies invest heavily in content distribution and have teams of people in place to support their business building activities. So it really is a wise choice to include publicity in your brand awareness strategy.

Ten-step plan to get publicity

STEP 1: *Become an expert.* Gain the appropriate skills and knowledge to become an expert in your field. No matter what your industry or calling – from being a creative through to coaching services – by developing a deep understanding and significant insight into your field, you are in a better position to stand out from everyone else when the media come calling. Gaining a deep understanding of your topic means that you will be able to develop content and clearly communicate your knowledge with confidence. Become a qualified member of your industry's association (if there is one) as this will give you credibility when the media choose to profile you. Belonging to an association of like-minded people (in which conferences and regular meetings are held) will aid you to gain further insight. Winning awards in your industry and gaining accreditation will add to your authority.

STEP 2: *Know what you want to communicate.* Be clear on what your message is and know what you want to say to the world. Understand that you need to have a point of difference or something interesting to say, and that you need to communicate that in an entertaining and informative way. Developing a strong point of view will set you apart from others in your field.

During your earlier personal branding work you will have uncovered your vision and perhaps a unique philosophy and belief system. By communicating that philosophy or being a true expert on a specialist topic, you will become sought after by the media. As an example, a speaker colleague of mine came up with the concept and based his business around "Thought Leaders". He may not have been the first person with this idea but it is his methodology that differentiates him.

"Sugar is bad for you" is a philosophy that has spurned numerous books and a big brand identity by another celebrity. My philosophy is that successful PR – creating "relationships" with your "public" – is built as a result of every encounter and impression you make.

Develop your unique take on your topic and summarise your message in short succinct, sound bites suitable for interviews or memes on social media.

STEP 3: *Find your audience.* You need to have an audience to listen to your message. In order to find your audience, conduct research into your ideal customer or client – perhaps a survey. Know your target audience well: their likes, dislikes, ambitions, fears, hobbies and interests. Aim to find out who your competitors are talking to and where they are gaining media coverage. Zero in on your target audience by creating compelling stories, articles and points of view around your topic that will appeal to them. It is important to think about "WIFT" – What Is In It For Them; your audience? What would they be interested to read or know about?

STEP 4: *Reach out to your target audience through the media.* Research the most appropriate magazines, newspapers, radio, online media or TV shows for your story. Build a database of media contacts. You can buy or subscribe to media directories that list an extensive range of media outlets or through your own research build a list of your top twenty to one hundred channels. Analyse your target audience. Do they read financial magazines or newspapers? Perhaps your audience enjoys reading small business magazines or weekly women's publications. Your local newspaper could be a good starting point. The first step is to purchase all of these magazines, then check in the front of the publication for the name of the editor as their contact details will usually be there. Next, call the newspapers and find out the name of the editor or chief reporter in order to begin building your own database of media contacts. This is a good starting point; however, you really need to research the right journalist for your industry and find out that person's contact details. It is off-putting for an editor to receive hundreds of media releases that are irrelevant to them. For example, if you are promoting health and wellness make sure you know who the health and wellness editors or journalists are.

I always prefer to be targeted and specific with my media distribution as it is imperative to follow through with journalists and editors. Conducting a successful publicity campaign takes considerable time and effort. Even if you only have your top ten journalists who you communicate with regularly, you still increase your chances of gaining valuable publicity exposure.

STEP 5: *Approach the media.* Send an email with your well-written media release. The main things to remember to include in your media release are the "five Ws": Who, What, When, Why and Where. We can add another "W" to that list – the Wow, the sizzle, the spin or the "USP". For me, the "USP" equates to the "unique shining point". USP usually stands for Unique Selling Proposition. In this instance, you are the selling point of this exercise. So what makes you shine? What is it about you or your product or service that stands out? What sets you out from the crowd? What is your angle and how can you define it simply and accurately? You must have something interesting to say that will position you as an expert in your field.

Write a catchy heading to include in the subject line of emails. Journalists and editors are very busy people so if the headline doesn't capture their attention they are unlikely to read any further (and certainly no further than the first paragraph).

Include a strong opening paragraph in your email. Sum up exactly what your story is in the first paragraph and ensure that you make it as interesting and compelling as possible. The most time-consuming part of writing a media release is coming up with a winning headline and first paragraph. This is really the vital part; it's the creative element where you should spend the most time and attention.

Your media release should also include an interesting quote from you. Quotes work well and are often used; however, they must be memorable and enhance the other information. At end of the release include a final paragraph that summarises you or your business. This is essentially your advertisement and so should include your website and any other contact information.

STEP 6: *Follow up.* Contact the journalists you've sent a media release to by phoning them if possible. You won't always make contact but it is essential to develop a method for following through and to be consistent with your media liaison. Developing a sense of confidence when talking to journalists may take time. However, like any good working relationship, it will develop with constant and clear communication.

"Make friends with journalists," was a tip I gleaned from an early mentor. And it turns out that some of them are really nice people! Of course, there are some people you will naturally gravitate to and others not so much. Learn to create and cultivate relationships with the media and they may help you to get what you want – which is exposure to their thousands of readers or viewers. One of the best ways to make friends in business or elsewhere is to meet in person. The days of the long lunch are in the past, but a quick coffee or breakfast to introduce yourself may work. Like most of us, journalists are busy people and don't always have the time to respond to emails, calls or invitations. Don't take this too personally. Your story might not be of interest this time but the next idea may work. If you do succeed with gaining media exposure, always thank the person who helped put you in the spotlight. Public relations is all about forming relationships with your public, and that includes the media.

Be persistent. Keep on submitting media releases and articles any time you have something interesting and relevant to say. But do learn to take no for an answer and don't be a pushy publicist. As previously mentioned, you need to build rapport and a professional working relationship with journalists, editors and producers in order to better understand and meet their needs. Not all your efforts will result in "free" publicity by mainstream media. However, there is still an advantage in creating content, articles and visual images as they can be used across your own media channels which, of course, is your website and social media accounts.

STEP 7: *Use images as "A picture tells a thousand words".* Media is entertainment and most people are attracted to strong visual images. That's why newspapers and magazines have eye-catching photographs on the cover page. Those captivating images help to sell this product. Send out a professional and creative photograph with your media release. Alternatively, when you ring the media outlet, you could suggest a photo opportunity. Better still, have a range of creative photos in various sizes available for download on your website. You could also have a branded USB memory stick that you send out or give to journalists when you meet them. If you are hoping to achieve television coverage, stage a creative film opportunity. Do this as early in the day as possible when the newsrooms, cameramen and photographers are not so busy. If you were holding an open day with lots of people attending, crack open a bottle of champagne on the front door. The handing over of the giant-sized cheque, or … I'll leave you to fill in the blanks. Creativity is the key.

STEP 8: *Be prepared for media interviews.* If you are lucky enough to be asked to appear on television, a video channel or do a radio interview; prepare possible questions beforehand

and rehearse the answers. It's a bit like a job interview process. You would never go to an interview without some idea of the answers you'd give to questions you might be asked. They may not ask you those questions; however, remember that you do know your topic better than they do so keep that in mind. Prepare two or three points you want to get across and try to keep on track with these points. For instance, make sure you get to mention the name of your book or project; don't just talk about it in general terms. Who is the book for and how does it help others? Think of sound bites and memorable phrases to convey. Go back to the information on networking and how you answer the, "What do you do?" question. It's the same principle when answering media questions. Keep your answers short and succinct with a bit of spark. They will simply ask you for more elaboration if required.

STEP 9: *Build up a portfolio of information about yourself.* When you do gain media coverage, you may choose to showcase it in a media room page on your website or have a branded USB with information about you. This is essentially your media kit, ready to send out to journalists. Your media room or media kit needs to have several components to it: a visual portrayal of who you are and written information. You need to include a short biography about yourself and your topics of expertise. This can simply be a paragraph or two about your business and you – the person behind the scenes. Next, list topics that you are able to comment on. Include any quotes or articles that may have already been used in the media to prove that you are an expert in this area. A simple one-page fact sheet with bullet points about your business is a good idea.

Now let's consider the visuals that you should be supplying. Include jpg images (low and high resolution) of yourself that can be downloaded, as well as your company logo. Rather than only having the stock standard headshot include a creative photo as well. The more options you can provide, the better the chance of having something appear in print. If you have any video footage of yourself or any audio recordings of any media interviews you have done, they can also be uploaded to your media room page. One thing to be aware of though is that having all this information available for public download may not be such a good idea from a privacy perspective – you never know where it may end up. I recommend that you either have it on USB for trusted media contacts or on a private area on your website to which you can direct journalists.

Journalists are like any other potential customer or client: they will do a search to find an expert in an area they need a comment on, to interview or write a story about. They may have already heard your name or come across you in a feature article while they've been doing other research. Perhaps they are prompted to find out more about you from a media release that you have sent them. They might Google your name or even your topic to find the right person to make a comment. Of course, journalists like to research so that they are armed with a lot of information before they conduct an interview.

STEP 10: *Consolidate your expertise.* Publish books, audio programs, DVDs and the like in order to be able to reap the rewards of successful publicity.

Use social media to shine

Let's now look at several social media platforms where you can engage with an audience and build your profile. This will not be news to you. Social media has had a significant impact on the way in which personal and professional brands are seen and heard these days.

LinkedIn, Facebook, YouTube, Instagram and Twitter are the channels I will concentrate on as they are the most prominent. Each social medium has its own particular characteristics and audiences. Having a presence across the major ones I believe will maximise your chances of standing out. However, it involves a lot of time and effort to leverage them all really well.

Before we get into the "nuts and bolts" of these social media channels, it is important to first address the need for a website and blog. If you're starting out you don't need to invest in a website or even a blog. However, as you progress on your journey of making a name for yourself you will definitely need to have both of these. Depending on your situation, a simple WordPress blog and website might be the solution. A bigger business may need a fully integrated CRM (Customer Relationship Management System) with the ability to send e-newsletters, a shopping cart system, and a much more advanced and sophisticated-looking website. IMPRESS*arios* can really do a lot to market themselves through other social media avenues before heading down this path.

Choose one or two social media sites and work these channels to your advantage. Take some time to think about your target audience. Who do you want to reach and what channel will be most suitable? You don't have to be across everything. Where are your prospective clients, employers or customers most likely to be? Start with one site until you have a reasonable number of followers – say about 1,000 people – then move on.

Your social media networks are a tool for you to express your ideas and showcase your skills and brand in front of those people who will make a difference for your business. The key is to determine your personal brand, story and theme so you can talk about it or display it on social media. What are the main messages you want to communicate and how do you communicate this information in a unique way across each social media platform? Keep this message consistent across the media, show your style and share your voice.

Of course, having fans and followers across different media is wonderful. However, the true essence of our marketing efforts is to build engagement and the relationships that eventually drive people to our door so they buy from us. For me and my business Shine Academy, my "door" is my email database. It takes marketing effort on my part through social media and publicity to get people to subscribe for that list but, once there, the potential to make a sale to them exponentially increases.

I mostly choose to do digital marketing through blogging and direct email to my online database. This strategy seems to work well for me and is part of my overall marketing mix. There's hundreds of ways of communicating with your target market and I could write another book on marketing alone – perhaps I might! But for now, let's keep our self-promotion efforts to the basics I have mentioned here.

LinkedIn

For most professionals working in a business environment and for emerging and established business leaders, LinkedIn is the "go to" social media channel of choice.

One common misconception about LinkedIn is that the only reason for being on the site is if you are looking for a job yourself or you are a recruiter looking for a candidate. Yes, there are many job seekers and recruiters on LinkedIn; however, anyone in business who wants to succeed should also be showcasing their brand and what they do. Whether you are an entrepreneur, CEO or a new to your industry, stating your brand position can open up possibilities and lead to new opportunities.

Try these tips to help your LinkedIn profile stand out.

1. **Headline.** Say what you do. Use four to six words which sum up your unique expertise. For example, Senior Branding Strategist, Business Coach to Executives, Event Manager, Travel Editor, Best Selling Author. Play it big. I suggest that you don't write your headline as Owner of XYZ Property Group or Founder of Ms CEO enterprises unless you are very well-known. Consider your headline as acting like real estate where you have the opportunity to spruik what you do.

2. **Headshot.** Your profile photograph is an important aid in making a strong first impression. Create visual impact by using a professionally photographed portrait image. People are viewing your page every day, so you do want to present a favourable visual image with a warm, welcoming expression. See Chapter Five for more detail on how to express your brand with captivating photographic images.

3. **Summary.** This is the first part of your content that will be read by others so it should sum up who you are and what you do in a compelling way. It includes what you are doing now or have done most recently so ensure that you convey this information with personality to your target market. Only the first two sentences are shown before people click through to

read further. Ensure these first sentences grab attention. To make the complete summary stand out, use paragraphs with headings and/or bullet points. Include all your specialties using your key words and include contact details. By keywords I mean the personal brand words or phrases you want to be known and found for.

4. **Activity.** Include interesting elements on your LinkedIn profile that will help you to stand out. Regularly share updates on items of interest to you and your target market. Share from online blogs or keep abreast of items of interest to post by signing up for Google alerts. Write your own articles and publish them as LinkedIn posts. Visual elements are eye-catching. Include videos, copies of publications, articles or books you have written, plus examples of certificates or awards. In addition, include logos of companies you have worked for. Keep active on your LinkedIn profile by searching for appropriate connections and regularly inviting people to connect with you.

5. **Credibility.** Back up your experience and expertise by including valuable third-party endorsements. Include recommendations from clients or former employers. Make sure your recommendations are relevant and only include endorsements of skills that you want to include. Don't have too many listed; just the ones you want to be known for. Make sure you list any accomplishments you have achieved and use keywords in your summary and descriptions that you want accredited to you as this will help optimise searches.

6. **Experience.** This is the part that looks more like a resume and details your experience and timeline.

Include everything relevant to you from your past work experience that highlights your knowledge, background and expertise. Factor in education, qualifications and additional experiences such as being involved with associations or boards. Don't just upload your resume; remember that LinkedIn is really a self-marketing tool. What do you really want to be known for?

A comprehensive LinkedIn profile will take time to write so I suggest doing that offline and only update your profile once you are completely satisfied. By the way, you can turn off your activity settings in your privacy controls so people will only see your updated activity when you have completed it.

Facebook

Currently, there's a lot of differing opinions on the best use of Facebook and a lot of differing experts who will ask you to sign up for their e-course on how to maximise its use. By all means, do this if you want to really get savvy with Facebook marketing. If you want to get specific and sell to a Facebook audience and do advertising, that is a whole other strategy. In this section, I will cover the basics of what you will need to do to gain Facebook followers.

At the end of the day, having tons of fans and followers across all social media is helping to grow awareness of you and your brand. Word of mouth is a powerful promotional tool. When I last looked at the statistics, Facebook in Australia has over 16,000,000 users. Given that the Australian population is around 24,500,000, it has massive penetration so it's definitely a worthwhile exercise to incorporate Facebook into your personal branding strategy.

Most of you will already have a personal page and you need that in order to set up a fan page or "like" page. Let's call it your business page as you are in the business of YOU – the IMPRESS*ario*. From your Facebook home page, go to your menu and set up your new business page. The process is quite simple and self-explanatory. You can choose to be a public figure or business or whatever is your most suitable category.

Once you have set up your business page; the idea is to move across any friends and family or clients from your personal page to your business page. First of all, you need to invite everyone you know to your personal page and build up your number of Facebook friends. Then send a request to them via your business page to "like" that page. This is the first step and, let's face it, not everyone will want to "like" your business page.

Engagement is key to getting "likes" on your business page. You need to be regularly posting blogs, photos, items of interest and videos. You want your posts to be share-worthy so others will share them, comment on and "like" them, and click on them as that will create more visits and more engagement.

Here are ten quick tips to get more Facebook followers:

1. Invite everyone you know to your Facebook personal page. Then once they are your Facebook friends, from your business page invite them to "like" that page. Do that regularly to keep growing your fan base.

2. Most of your friends won't be interested in your business page. However, some of your target audience might find you through this process, so don't post anything on your personal page that may lead to embarrassment further down the track. Set up your

personal information and privacy settings the way in which you want your profile to appear. In the "About" section, do put a link on your personal page to your business page, so fans will find you.

3. Create and upload a well-designed cover photo that is 851 x 351 pixel dimensions. This image may be a photo of you in action or some simple example of what you and your business are all about. This cover image could be updated if you are doing an upcoming event and include a call to action or a "buy now" button or a "click here" button which links back to additional information on your website (if you have one).

4. Make use of all the different sections of your business page. Include a great welcome video and add in apps such as Twitter or Instagram. Complete the "About You" section, your contact details and anything else that may be relevant to your audience.

5. Start posting! Make it interesting, entertaining and fun. Posts that add value to others will gain more "likes" and shares. Mix up your type of posts and make them real by showcasing your personality. Include photos of you at work, with other people at work, having fun at work, or doing something such as volunteering for a good cause. Photos get the most shares and people also like quotes and videos. People always love the quirky cat and dog videos! But, seriously, think creatively and come up with posts that will be of interest.

6. Include a "call to action" on your posts such as; "remember to share" or "hope you like and share". Or ask a question to try to elicit responses. You can also ask your fans to visit your website and include your website details or a link to a blog or certain page. And

if people do comment, you need to be ready to answer and interact with your audience. Keep the interaction going by "liking" and commenting on influencers and client's posts.

7. Facebook gives an insight into who you are and may spark interest with prospects. Another tip is to add the "like my Facebook page" social plugin box on your website and blog. People who visit may want to get to know you first through Facebook. As you continue to develop that relationship, with interesting engagement (and a bit of luck!), they will go from stranger to prospect and may eventually engage with you through your website and become a customer.

8. One way to find out what posts work well with your audience is to visit others' Facebook pages. Do your research. Once you have a few followers, see what other pages they like and the type of posts that are getting attention. Check out your competition or those in a similar field. Have a look and see what type of posts are being liked and shared; what are their fans talking about?

9. Once you understand what fans are engaged by and talking about, you can come up with a content marketing plan. This might consist of a quote one day, followed the next day by a photo of you in action, followed by a video or blog. Mix it up and post at least a few days per week. Be mindful of overly promotional posts that are all about your business. They will receive less priority in the News Feed, which is where you need to be to grow your "likes".

10. Advertising is the next step to building your followers. Experiment with boosting or simple page advertising to grow your fan base. The more you do this the more

traffic you will generate to your page. Once you get to about 1,000 followers, do paid advertising to promote a particular product or service. This is the quickest way to grow more fans and get more likes.

Other communication channels

I have highlighted LinkedIn and Facebook as the two most prominent social media channels for a business person to use. Now these two options may be irrelevant if you are selling travel or bikinis. In this case, Instagram could be your medium of choice. What I suggest you do is to conduct research for your personal brand, business and the audience you want to engage with and utilise that communication channel or choose a couple of them, predominantly. Align your brand look across all your channels, including your website and other communication collateral such as business cards, post-cards, newsletters and anything else that reflects your brand. In summary, the few I have selected to highlight are the most widely used. Other channels of communication could be pod-casts, webinars, teleseminars and so on it goes …

YouTube

YouTube is the second largest search engine in the world, so it would be crazy not to utilise it in your overall promotional strategy. But having videos on YouTube is not relevant for everyone. It suits my business and my personal branding approach. As an IMPRESS*ario,* I do recommend incorporating YouTube into your marketing mix.

As with Facebook and LinkedIn, having a well-designed header banner will help capture attention and tell the story of YOU.

You may already subscribe to certain YouTube channels yourself and have probably looked up a "how to do it" video on YouTube in the past. There are numerous success stories of business owners who make a very lucrative living from YouTube by advertising content on their channels. Just search for the term "cupcake" and see what comes up! The thing these success stories with millions of followers and views all have in common is that they have a clearly defined niche. Regardless of whether it's cupcakes, makeup, digital marketing or gaming, they have all honed-in on that one thing. Your "thing" and your brand should be communicated on YouTube to create a following and, ultimately, to make it easier for people to find you and work with you.

With YouTube, there's a variety of communication styles and production styles to choose from: studio productions, in your office or home with a simple iPhone and selfie stick, on location – you name it someone is doing it! That choice is up to you and your budget. The key is to keep it real; let your true essence emanate since that will appeal to viewers. To captivate your audience and have them wanting to visit your channel often, you need to provide something that is relevant to them. It is important not to be too "salesy"; provide a solution to their problem or enlighten them in some way with your knowledge. YouTube is current currency; it is where people will get to know you.

Again, there is so much information online, I don't need to go into detail here except to suggest that you "Just do it"!

Twitter

I was in two minds when considering whether or not to include Twitter in this line-up. It is widely used in many countries and some people swear by it as a means of growing your brand. Like the other social media channels, if used well it can be a great communication tool. It is another outlet to post your blogs and announcements but the real key to engagement on Twitter is authenticity and conversation. It takes time and work to tweet often and to be authentic. You really need to consider if this is time you are willing to invest and if this is the right social media channel for you.

If you choose to include Twitter in your social media mix, you might like to try these few ideas. Search and follow experts and leaders who are in a similar industry to yours and engage in the commentary around your particular topic. Respond to the tweets that are of interest to you and "like" and share them. When you do post a blog or comment, use #hashtags that are relevant keywords for your post to optimise your tweet being found in searches.

As always on social media, be yourself. Sharing your opinions and feelings will help you to build a more engaged Twitter following. Also, voicing your unique point of view and displaying a sense of humour will shine through. Keep your tweets upbeat and post about the great things that are happening in your life or business.

Instagram

I'm fascinated by Instagram and waste way too much time looking through the interesting and creative photographs and visuals that are posted. And this is the key – to be interesting and creative to capture people's attention. Whether you are posting well-designed images with a meaningful quote or uploading photos of yourself in the latest fashion, travel or lifestyle pictures, they need to be relevant to your brand story.

Instagram is perfect for reflecting the visual expression of your personal brand and it is where you can share more insight into who you are, including your lifestyle, hobbies or interests. Engagement by following, liking and commenting on other posts is one key to growing your own Instagram following. To create further influence, be creative with your Feed by perhaps choosing a theme or a colour block or certain style and be consistent with that in your posts. Influencers with millions of followers who are not mainstream celebrities have been created through using Instagram. You too can become a major influencer and paint the picture of the IMPRESS*ario* you are by learning to use Instagram well.

Creating a name for yourself does take time and commitment and the conviction that it is worth the effort. Yes, it is! I hope to see your name in the spotlight one day.

Publicist to the star – Action plan

You are the "star" in your own show. Be your own publicist by writing and issuing interesting media releases.

Compile your media contact list, and then contact or call and create connections.

Research and use the social media channels that will help you to shine.

Nine

The Show Must Go On

"The Show Must Go On!"

– Anonymous

It's Show Time, folks! You have finally made a name for yourself. You've passed the audition stages and landed that great gig. Or you have been selected for the team. Perhaps your years of training have helped you to land a stage role. Or your start-up organisation or business expertise is beginning to shine through. Now is not the time to back away. The sweet smell of success might be hindered by any display of nerves or fear at this point.

We all feel it, yet as the saying goes "Feel the fear and do it anyway". I remember on one occasion going white water rafting and feeling very nervous. The further we travelled into the hinterland to get to the launch point for the canoes, the more anxious I became; I was almost having a panic attack. I literally wanted to get off the bus and walk back home. It was irrational fear. It is always the anticipation before a big event that pushes the adrenalin to its highest.

My husband could see what was going on and said to me, "Turn the fear into excitement". He also reassured me that we were in safe hands and nothing was going to go wrong. In the end, I did the canoe trip – and loved it! My sense of accomplishment at the finish was almost as exhilarating as the trip itself.

Turn the fear into excitement

This is not the only time I have felt panicky. I have suffered from panic attacks and anxiety and have learned techniques to manage this condition, which tends to come and go. Be reassured if you feel this way sometimes; you are not alone. It is the natural fear or flight response to stressful situations. My first experience of a panic attack was overwhelming. I was "fleeing" a toxic relationship and moving interstate. I stayed with my parents the night before taking the long road trip and, although I was in a totally safe environment, it suddenly hit me! As I was drifting off to sleep, my heart started racing, my breath seemed to escape and I started hyperventilating. I felt as though I needed to escape from the room immediately. I didn't know what was happening to me and I felt horrible. However, the feeling passed and I started my trip the next day as planned. It wasn't just a "one-off" though and, for me and many other people, it is a condition that must be managed. And it can be. There has been so much research, study and books and articles written about anxiety disorders and phobias. So it is a very real condition and should not be dismissed lightly in the few sentences I have written here. I am not a psychologist or therapist and so it is not my place to tell you how to overcome your irrational fears if this is what you are truly facing. All I can say here is that I have experienced this condition myself so I know that, with some professional help and learned techniques, you can get through it as well.

Confronting situations will always be an aspect of our lives, regardless of whether they are unexpected (such as facing the loss of a loved one) or planned (such as giving a public speaking presentation for the first time). Not everyone will have irrational fears associated with these events, but a lot of people will experience extreme nervousness.

Being anxious in situations where you need to be on show can hold you back from achieving your goals. For instance, having a job interview or doing a presentation, media interview or any sort of performance where you (and your expertise) are under scrutiny can be daunting. I often work with clients one-to-one on their presentation skills. Invariably, they tell me that the Number One obstacle they experience is nerves and how to overcome them. It is a very real fear for many people. There is even a special word for it – "Glossophobia" which means "fear of speaking in public". Even seasoned performers will experience some level of nervousness on certain occasions; however, that extra rush of adrenalin can also boost a performance. I don't think we can completely eradicate nerves, but you also don't want them to become such a distraction that they become the only thing you focus on. You need to put fear or nervousness into its right perspective.

I told my personal story for the first time – the one I have shared in this book about my teenage pregnancy – to an audience of over ninety businesswomen (where my daughter was also in attendance). It was one of the most nerve-wracking experiences I have ever been through. Not that anyone else would really have noticed as it was the anticipation and anxiety leading up to the event which I found most daunting. I experienced a couple of sleepless nights during which

I thought about all the horrible things that could happen. I could faint; the audience might laugh at me; or think I'm a bad person. I might forget my lines or worse. What would they say if I just didn't turn up? You name it, I imagined it. Of course, none of that occurred. The intense fear subsided once I was at the location, dressed and ready, and in performance mode. I was also well-prepared by relaxing beforehand with meditation in order to visualise a successful outcome. I directed my focus on why my story might be of interest to the audience – what was in it for them? I also decided they would be more likely to be friendly and supportive if I mingled, shook hands and chatted with people, prior to getting up on stage to speak. All of those tactics helped me to feel in control and not overwhelmed throughout my talk. I felt ready for the presentation, so I always recommend that one of the best ways to handle nerves is to be well-prepared.

Rehearse, rehearse and rehearse. Practise your speech and plan the best responses to questions you may be asked at an interview. Practise how you will answer those questions. Do a mock interview with a friend and answer your questions out loud. Rehearse your presentation in front of friends. You may be tempted to just "wing it" as you want to come across to your audience as being natural and spontaneous. That is, of course, the desired response; to appear as though the talk or interview is effortless yet interesting. Story telling in particular is not about memorising the words but, rather, to memorise the experience and tell it in the same way that it happened. You also need to inform, entertain and keep on track with your messages so the audience – of one or many – can follow what you're saying. There is nothing worse than listening to someone who goes from one tangent to another without being able to grasp the gist of what they are talking about. Actors' lines are delivered to the writer's script to ensure the story is told according to their vision, and those lines must be learned. Spontaneity, ad lib and performance technique is added in to enhance the final delivery. That is not to say an actor (experienced or otherwise) does not feel nervous sometimes on opening night or the first day on set. It is their years of study, preparation and practise that help them with those pre-show jitters.

Performers also like to stretch themselves: to do something new, try a different type of role or stage a new rock concert based on their latest recording. Of course, they feel nervous putting themselves "out there" to be scrutinised, criticised or applauded. And that is what makes stand out performers unique; the ability to keep on going year after year with something new and then following up with another show or song.

If it is to be, it's up to me

There are many "one hit wonders". Luck can play a part when one book or song takes off and sells millions of copies. The follow-up album might not work but most stars don't give up at this point; they keep performing or producing and coming up with their next idea. Jim Weatherly is the songwriter of *The Best Thing That Ever Happened to Me* which was a huge hit in the 1970s and has since been recorded by a number of artists. I know the song and like it, although I'd never heard of the songwriter until recently. I read that Weatherly wrote the song for his father-in-law as a present to his wife. Apparently, the song came to him in a stream of consciousness and took only about thirty minutes or so to write. It "just happened", however, he didn't rest on his laurels and continued to write songs – some were hits and some not.

If you listen closely to the lyrics of the song you may think the songwriter was attributing this success to someone else. Remember, the YOU in IMPRESS*ario* is ... you. Outside influences such as friends, family and fans may help you to get lucky and succeed; however, you are the one who performs on opening night and beyond.

Your opening night might be a new business, a book, or your first media appearance and it is normal to feel some sort of trepidation. Yet, it gets easier with practise and time. The key is that you need to repeat the process. Follow up and follow on with your next move. Not "rinse and repeat" which is the same old action repeated over and over. It might work once or even several times. However, you need to be willing to try something new; stretch to reach your potential and give your fans another reason to engage with you.

Easier said than done I know and it does take commitment, faith and confidence on your part, which can come and go. We are only human after all.

The thing is though, as you grow and learn, you will also have something else to say and share with your audience. You will discover a new slant on your topic or new position. By feeling energised and inspired about what you do, you will always produce something that adds value to your target market and develops your own sense of accomplishment.

A well-known example is Jamie Oliver, who is described as being a celebrity chef and restaurateur. He started out as a pastry chef after first gaining credentials at cooking school and experience working in his parent's pub. He did get a "lucky break" when working at The River Café in London; he was talent spotted by the BBC when he appeared in a documentary about the restaurant. His first television show *The Naked Chef* aired in 1999 and, a short while later, his first cook book *The Naked Chef* was published. But it wasn't luck that kept him going … and still going almost twenty years later. It was dedication, hard work, talent, grit and a share of successes and failures.

As a result of his early years of hard work, Jamie Oliver has released a range of cook books; television shows with different themes; openings and closings of restaurants; and a movement spawned by cooking and eating healthier meals. He continually comes up with something new: the follow up. Whether it is *Jamie's 30-Minute Meals, Jamie's 15-Minute Meals, Jamie's Kitchen, Jamie's Italy, Jamie's Comfort Food* or *Super Food*, he constantly delivers new product for his fans and the public at large.

The second act

Your opening night is just the starting point. You've taken a bow and you feel the flush of excitement; you have succeeded. Oh, but now I have to do it all over again? Well, yes – day after day you have to keep turning up and tuning in. Can you imagine what it must be like for the Rolling Stones to perform *Start Me Up* over and over? In fact, they have been playing and opening concerts with that song since 1981. The longest running play on London's West End is *Mousetrap* and, now in its 65th year, it is still going strong. One of the actors, David Raven is in the *Guinness Book of Records* as "The Most Durable Actor" for giving 4,575 performances in the same role.

These people keep going because they are passionate and love what they do. Not all circumstances in our lives will be something we enjoy. Resilience in tough times and having faith that things will work out is what helps keep people moving forward. In business and in "the play of life", we will continue to be tested. Fronting up each day to face the world can affect a lot of people; depression, sickness and poverty are rife throughout the world. Most of you reading this book will be privileged to live in a world where we do have choice – notwithstanding any freak accidents or occurrences, of course. However, "Shit happens", as they say. It is how we choose to front up each time that determines our outcome.

The world of work has changed forever and today many more people than previously are forgoing the traditional route of working for employers and forging an entrepreneurial path – either by choice or necessity. In my forty plus years of working, I've had a few jobs but I've mostly worked for myself. In the past, I was described as a freelancer. These days, it seems as though everyone is an entrepreneur and I think that's great.

We are the producers and directors of our own work and life, and we need to make life work. IMPRESS*arios* recognise that "life is long". The average life expectancy for both male and female Australians is 82.8 years, as reported by the World Health Organisation in 2015. That means we have a lot of living to do, and will most likely want to work and play to the utmost.

Older age should not be a barrier to achieving your dreams. Encore entrepreneurs are popping up everywhere and, through the ages, many older people have reinvented and pursued second act careers. The late US actress, Kathryn Joosten won two Emmy Awards (in 2005 and 2008) for her role in the television show *Desperate Housewives*. Kathryn didn't start acting until she was forty-two, following her previous career as a psychiatric nurse. It still took her ten years from that point to start to get small parts in TV shows, proving once again that it can take ten years to be an "overnight success." Yet, if you persevere, your dream can come true. Kathryn was in her 60s when she was awarded an Emmy.

Leading Australian actor, Geoffrey Rush was forty-four and had been working as an actor for twenty-five years before he hit the "big time" with his Academy Award winning role in the movie *Shine*. One of Australia's long-standing, successful businesswomen – Diana Williams – founded the fitness centre franchise, Fernwood Fitness in 1989 when she was in her forties.

Personally, I'm excited about the increased presence of older women in the fashion and beauty industry. There is still a long way to go; however, it is encouraging to see major consumer brands showcasing famous mature actresses such as Jane Fonda and Helen Mirren, as well as prominent 1960s teenage model "Twiggy" as the face of their products. These women are "famous faces", of course, but even in Australia, women I once worked with as a young model are still gracing the pages of our glossy magazines.

Your dream may be to become a "grey nomad" and travel the countryside. Yet, you will still be using your grey matter to learn to drive the 4WD vehicle, navigate the roads and be stimulated by new places and sights. That's what it is all about; the show must go on and be lived to the full.

Enjoy the spotlight

It is now opening night … or the equivalent for you. Whatever you set out to achieve has come to fruition, and there you are waiting in the wings for the curtain to rise. This is the moment to savour. You have done it. All eyes are on you. You know that this is your moment in the spotlight. And you have prepared and worked so hard for it. At this point, which is the culmination of all your practise and preparation, you commit to your performance. This is the "real deal"; when your well-honed technique combines with passion and the sparks really start to fly. Enjoy it!

Your moment might not be one that is applauded by an audience – but you do have your fans. Let them enjoy the spotlight with you. People love going to the cinema or theatre to see a performance, whether it is by a famous actor or a motivational speaker. We want to be in their limelight and experience that aura for a short time. It lifts all of us up and takes us away from the mundane to a place of fantasy or inspiration. Your supporters and fans want you to succeed. They want to experience a bit of that glitter or sparkle that you radiate, so be gracious to others along the way. We can't do it alone. Having a team around you makes it possible; make it count for them too.

Don't let turkeys get you down

Not all of your family and friends will be supportive; there will be some people who may be envious of your position or success. Others could try to undermine you. This is where your self-belief needs to kick in. You've made it this far so "don't let the turkeys get you down", which is what a former boss of mine used to say. We all have bad days; that is only natural. Some days and events and people will test you more than others. Of course, fans who bask in your glow may also build you up to the point where you believe you are god's gift to the world and "better than sliced bread" (to use an Australian colloquialism) It is not so.

Don't believe all the hype. You may have glowing reviews one day and not so positive ones the next. There will always be others on social media who appear to "have it all" and be doing so much better than you. Criticism and negative feedback on anything – particularly if you've poured your heart and soul into it – can be tough. It is also wise to just acknowledge it and get a second opinion. Feedback from several sources may give you a more balanced viewpoint.

It is important to keep a level head. Have confidence in your ability and self-belief but don't be a diva or divo. Be kind to those who treat you well on the way up and, perhaps if your star does start to dip a little, they will still be supportive of you on the way down. Life has a way of taking twists and turns and a true IMPRESS*ario* will be able to manage the various fluctuations and changing landscape.

It is the little things that count and there is a range of ways of demonstrating your appreciation of others: perhaps a simple word of thanks, a thank you gift, a card or well thought out letter. Be thankful and gracious. Respect other people's role in your life, and recognise their time and effort. Acknowledge the applause. Performers will take a bow at the end of their act. Designers will walk the runway with their models, allowing the audience to show their appreciation. Let them. Sign the books and pose with fans for selfies. Perhaps not literally, but pause for that moment before your next move to accept the compliment and say thank you.

There are many people who inspire me and whose success I applaud. The lovely people who wrote testimonials for this book are all successful in their own right and have forged their own path, despite their often difficult choices or life circumstances.

What does your path and destiny hold? I do hope you have the necessary conviction to forge on and become the producer of your plan for your future.

Being the star of your own show – whether it's as a housewife, superstar or CEO – is all about emanating confidence, dignity and a touch of pizazz. Let's think what pizazz is: spark or zest and energy. When your preparation meets opportunity that is when you will truly shine.

Go ahead, be the IMPRESS*ario* who makes a grand impression on the world!

Conclusion

Keep shining

Congratulations on taking the first step in presenting and promoting the star within you. Having completed reading IMPRESS*ario,* you will have a better understanding and an outline of the steps you need to take to develop your personal brand and stand out in business. So now it's over to you …

My wish is that you don't just read this book; rather, that you follow through with the actions outlined in the exercises and heed the advice I have put forward. I truly believe that taking a detailed step-by-step approach to building your brand and business will be a sure-fire way for you to gain the success you desire. You don't have to be a carbon copy of someone else – you have what it takes to cultivate the best version of you. Delve deep to uncover the authentic, real, engaging and inspiring you, and shine brightly.

Plans don't always go the way we hope, of course. But if you do stay on course and keep referring to the process I have outlined in IMPRESS*ario,* then even if you do go off track from time to time, you will eventually reach a satisfying outcome.

I hope my book inspires you as an entrepreneur or woman in business to take a confident stand, showcase your personal best and shine. And to encourage those of you who may be harbouring past negative experiences and limiting your success by "getting in your own way". I also hope that my words will serve to bolster up-and-coming entrepreneurs. Most long-term success is achieved by those who persevere, and who are able to pick themselves up and start all over again, regardless of what happens.

I'd love to make a difference to you and your future so that you become an IMPRESS*ario*. My long-term goal is to spread the word of personal branding to thousands of people through my book, and through my consulting and speaking business. If you have been inspired to learn more and take further action, then please get in touch. You can read more about my programs below or visit my website: www.suecurrie.com.au

About Sue Currie programs

At Sue Currie and Shine Academy we hope that you now feel inspired to become the IMPRESS*ario* of your brand and business.

The tools, tips and worksheets within this book will help you plan, produce and work towards a successful outcome. However, if you want to go that extra step and gain further encouragement, free video training is available on the Sue Currie website (www.suecurrie.com.au) for you to download.

This series of videos will give you insight into your "Nook, Look and Hook – 3 Simple Steps to Build a Stand Out Personal Brand".

Individual programs

Our website – suecurrie.com.au – also offers an online program to guide you to discover and develop your stand-out, impressive brand. The Shine Personal Branding program takes you through a detailed, step-by-step approach as outlined in IMPRESS*ario*. With personal coaching and support, this is the ideal program to help you to establish your entrepreneurial brand.

Corporate programs

Sue Currie helps business owners and corporate executives create lucrative connections with clients by delivering workshops and professional development to elevate you or your team's personal brand, professional image, presentation brand and public profile. By developing a confident, clear brand presence, your influence and profit will be enhanced. For more information, inquire at www.suecurrie.com.au.

Speaking

Recognised as Australia's leading personal branding speaker, Sue Currie has a wealth of knowledge in her field. Sue's hands-on approach to building an outstanding personal brand and making an indelible impression has resulted in great success for her clients. Audience comments include: *Engaging … thought provoking … shared value … practical advice … dynamic …*

Sue presents Australia wide and internationally. She has been a keynote speaker at numerous conferences, including Meetings and Events Australia Convention, Filex Convention, Westpac Alfred Davidson Awards, Chartered

Accountants Business Forum, Gartner Security and Risk Management Summit, Asia Professional Speakers Summit, Association of Image Consultants International Conference and has delivered speaking and training programs to organisations such as AMP, Cerebos, Fuji Xerox, GSK, KPMG and Reckitt Benckiser.

For media inquiries or to book Sue Currie for your conference or event, call 1300 723 713 or visit the website – www.suecurrie.com.au.

Bibliography

Books

Everett, Lesley (2004) *Walking Tall: Key Steps to Total Image Impact*, Lesley Everett, Bracknell.

Peters, Tom (1999) *The Brand You 50 (Reinventing Work): Fifty Ways to Transform Yourself from an "Employee" into a Brand That Shouts Distinction, Commitment, and Passion!* Knopf, New York.

Stanislavski, Constantin (1980) *An Actor Prepares*, Eyre Methuen Ltd, London.

Stanislavski, Constantin (1989) *Building a Character*, Routledge/Theatre Arts Books, New York.

Luft, J. & Ingham, H. (1955) *The Johari Window: A Graphic Model of Interpersonal Awareness*.

Montoya, Peter; Vandehey, Tim (2005) *The Brand Called You: The Ultimate Personal Branding Handbook to Transform Anyone into an Indispensable Brand*, Montoya, USA.

Thompson, Larry A., (2005) *Shine: A Powerful 4-Step Plan for Becoming a Star in Anything You Do*, McGraw-Hill, New York.

Henderson, Robyn (2004) *How to Master Networking*, Sea Change Publishing, Kingscliff.

Quotes

Allen, Woody, *Eighty percent of success is showing up.*
http://www.nytimes.com/1989/08/13/magazine/on-language-the-elision-fields.html

Zanuck, Richard D. *Star quality is one of the most difficult things to describe. It emanates from the person, and he may not even understand it himself. It's a quality that separates the star from the rest of us.*
http://articles.latimes.com/1998/mar/22/opinion/op-31419

De Laurentiis, Dino, *If no producer, no movie.*
http://www.theglobeandmail.com/arts/de-laurentiis-keeps-the-films-rolling/article4139804/

Barnum, P.T. *Without promotion, something terrible happens. Nothing!*
https://en.wikipedia.org/wiki/P._T._Barnum

Turner, Ted, *Early to bed, early to rise, work like hell and advertise!*
http://www.tedturner.com/books/

Further Reading

Association of Image Consultants International
www.aici.org
Johari Window
https://en.wikipedia.org/wiki/Johari_window
360º Reach
http://www.reachpersonalbranding.com/

Richard Branson
https://www.virgin.com/entrepreneur/richard-branson-
even-introverts-can-become-great-entrepreneurs

Style Book
www.stylebookapp.com

Closet Space
www.closetspace.com

The Imposter Syndrome
www.wikipedia.org/wiki/Impostor_syndrome

About the Author

Sue Currie is a businesswoman, speaker, author, consultant, educator and media personality. She is widely recognised as being an authority on personal branding to boost people's image, brand and business.

Sue is the founder and leading light behind Shine Academy; providing education, consulting and professional development training on personal branding and public profile solutions to help businesses and entrepreneurs position themselves and present an influential professional brand.

Sue Currie knows that any business involves more than just delivering a message. It is about really living it … and she *walks her talk*. Sue has spent many years in the public eye – on camera, on the platform and behind the scenes. From an early start as a fashion model and TV presenter, to Vice President of PR and Communications in a corporate environment, and finally to running her successful consulting business, Sue's whole career has been about helping others to enhance their image, and build their reputation, credibility and recognition, by harnessing personal and professional public relations skills in order to shine.

As a result of her media profile, practical experience and business success, Sue is considered to be a leading authority on personal branding, having worked with hundreds of clients in the areas of keynote speaking, professional development training and public image consultancy. Her client list ranges from Top 100 Companies, to leading Associations and SMEs.

Sue has appeared on *Sky News Business,* in magazines and newspapers such as *Business Review Weekly, Vogue, Cleo, Marketing Magazine, Dynamic Business, Daily Telegraph, The Sydney Morning Herald, The Age* and on Qantas Q Radio.

Sue aims to inspire entrepreneurs and women in business to take a confident stand, showcase their personal best and shine.